Trade in Counterfeit Products and the UK Economy

FAKE GOODS, REAL LOSSES

OECD
BETTER POLICIES FOR BETTER LIVES

Please cite this publication as:
OECD (2017), *Trade in Counterfeit Products and the UK Economy: Fake Goods, Real Losses*, OECD Publishing, Paris.
http://dx.doi.org/10.1787/9789264279063-en

ISBN 978-92-64-27905-6 (print)
ISBN 978-92-64-27906-3 (PDF)

Photo credits: Cover Illustration © Jeffrey Fisher.

Corrigenda to OECD publications may be found on line at: *www.oecd.org/about/publishing/corrigenda.htm*.

Preface

The UK is an example of a modern, innovation-based economy whose success relies on its ability to maximise the value of, and protect, its intellectual property rights (IPRs). The economy is well integrated globally, through active participation in global value chains. A consequence of its high IP-intensity is its potential vulnerability to counterfeiting and piracy on the global stage.

To effectively address the threat of counterfeit trade, it is essential to precisely measure its scale, scope and impact, and to identify any governance gaps that increase vulnerability. This study assesses the negative impacts of counterfeit trade on UK rights holders and on the UK government, and provides methodologies for determining the areas of governance of IP enforcement that need strengthening.

We are confident this study provides an excellent basis to inform and develop policy to tackle the growing threat of counterfeiting and piracy in the United Kingdom

Pippa Hall

Director of Innovation and Chief Economist,
UK Intellectual Property Office

Rolf Alter

Director,
OECD/GOV

Foreword

The modern structure of the UK economy is largely based on knowledge, ideas and innovation. The innovative industries that rely on intellectual property (IP) rights (including trademarks) are the backbone of the UK economy. These industries are also an integral part of global value chains, which make the UK a significant contributor of value added in the complex structures of world trade.

The trademark-intensive UK economy and its active participation in global value chains help boost the country's economic growth. At the same time, these factors make it highly susceptible to trade in counterfeit goods.

The risk of trade in counterfeits has been growing in recent years, not only becoming a significant threat to the engine of economic growth, but also undermining good governance, the rule of law and citizens' trust in government. As shown by the recent OECD reports, *Trade in Counterfeit and Pirated Goods: Mapping the Economic Impact* and *Mapping the Real Routes of Trade in Fake Goods*, trade in counterfeit and pirated goods amounted to up to 2.5 % of world trade in 2013, and was an even higher share (5%) of imports into the EU. Parties that engage in counterfeit trade are well organized, and ship goods via very complex routes that pose a formidable challenge for enforcement authorities.

Trade in counterfeit goods negatively affects UK rights holders, the UK government, and the reputation of UK firms. For the UK government, counterfeiting and piracy has an impact on tax revenues, and supports an expansion of organized criminal networks that are often actively involved in counterfeit and pirated trade. The study finds that counterfeit goods accounted for as much as 4% of total imports to the UK. At the same time, fakes make up at least 3%

of the total value of products with UK trademarks and patents that are traded worldwide.

The consequences are significant. The estimated total volume of sales lost by UK rights owners due to counterfeiting amounted to almost 2 % of their total sales in 2013. Furthermore, in 2013 an estimated sixty thousand jobs were lost in the UK due to the threat of counterfeiting (about 1.15% of total UK employment). Lastly, for the UK government, counterfeiting may have resulted in a potential loss of almost GBP 3.8 billion in tax revenue.

In order to design effective policies to tackle the threat of counterfeit trade in the UK context, the problem needs to be identified and assessed. This study serves two purposes:

It proposes an objective and fact-based methodology for such quantitative assessment of the scale and harmful effects of counterfeit trade on UK rights holders and the UK government;

It applies this methodology, providing robust findings that will help the UK government design policies to combat counterfeiting and piracy and to identify the main governance gaps in this area.

This study was carried out by the OECD's Task Force on Countering Illicit Trade. The Task Force is part of the OECD High Level Risk Forum, which focuses on evidence-based research and advanced analytics to assist policy makers in mapping and understanding the market vulnerabilities exploited and created by illicit trade. This is the first of a set of country and regional case studies that will not only assess the scale and magnitude of counterfeit trade, but also quantify some of its negative economic impacts at a regional level.

The report was prepared by Piotr Stryszowski, Senior Economist, and Florence Mouradian, Economist at the OECD Directorate for Public Governance and Territorial Development, under the supervision of Stéphane Jacobzone, Counsellor, OECD.

The authors wish to thank Mary-Anne Venables, Economic Advisor at the UKIPO for her invaluable contribution to this study. The authors would also like to thank Pippa Hall, David Humphries and Thomas Walkden from the UKIPO for their useful insights.

The authors are grateful to participants of several seminars and workshops for their valuable assistance provided.

The OECD Secretariat wishes to thank Liv Gaunt, Marie-Claude Gohier, Fiona Hinchcliffe and Andrea Uhrhammer for their editorial and production support.

The quantitative research in this study relied on a rich global database on customs seizures, provided by the World Customs Organization (WCO) and supplemented with regional data submitted by the European Commission's Directorate-General for Taxation and Customs Union, the US Customs and Border Protection Agency and the US Immigration and Customs Enforcement. The authors express their gratitude for the data and for the valuable support of these institutions.

Table of contents

Figures

Tables

Boxes

Executive summary

Trade in counterfeit goods is a longstanding socio-economic problem that continues to grow in scope and magnitude. It gives rise to significant challenges to effective governance, efficient business and the well-being of consumers, while simultaneously being a key source of income for organised criminal groups.

For consumers, counterfeiting poses dangers for health, safety and privacy. It may also lower consumer satisfaction, notably when low-quality fake goods are purchased unknowingly. For intellectual property rights holders and their authorised vendors, rising counterfeiting brings revenue losses, while trademark infringements continuously erode brand value. For governments, counterfeiting means lost tax revenues, higher unemployment and greater expenses in ensuring compliance with anti-counterfeiting legislation, and in reacting to public safety threats and labour-market distortions.

This report measures the direct, economic effects of counterfeiting on consumers, retail and manufacturing industry and governments in the United Kingdom (UK). It does so from two perspectives: (1) the impacts on these three groups of imports of fake products into the UK; and (2) the impact on UK intellectual property rights holders of the global trade in fake products. The study developed a methodology to gauge the magnitude and scale of counterfeit trade in the UK and to quantify its direct economic impact. It relied primarily on a unique international set of customs seizure data, as well as structured interviews with trade and customs experts.

The results of this study refer to 2013 – the year for which latest data are available. However the methodology could be re-used to determine the scale of harm caused by counterfeiting on the UK economy once the new data become available.

Key findings

Trade in counterfeit goods – the UK context

- Imports of counterfeit goods to the UK accounted for as much as GBP 9.3 billion in 2013. This represents 4% of UK imports, well above the 2.5% average share of fake goods in world imports. Electronic and electrical equipment, clothing and footwear were the most frequent counterfeit products smuggled into the UK, followed by toys and games, and leather goods.
- Fakes make up at least 3% of the total value of products with trademarks and patents of UK residents that are traded worldwide. However, for some product categories, like toys, clothing and footwear, this share exceeds 10%.
- China and Hong Kong (China) and India are the main sources of counterfeit imports to the UK. Asian economies, particularly China, India and Turkey are the main provenance of counterfeit and pirated goods that infringe the IPRs of UK residents.
- Approximately half (48%) of counterfeit and pirated were intended for sale on the secondary market. These fake goods were supposed to deceive consumers, who would have bought them believing these goods were genuine.

Impacts on the UK

- **Impacts on sales:** The total volume of lost sales of genuine products in the UK wholesale and retail sector due to imported counterfeit and pirated substitutes amounted to GBP 4.218 billion in 2013, equivalent to 1.37% of total sales in the sector that year. The total volume of lost sales by UK IP rights owners amounted to GBP 8.6 billion, or 1.95% of their total sales in 2013.
- **Impacts on consumers:** The total consumer detriment (the price premium unjustly paid by the consumer in the belief that they are buying a genuine product) of buying counterfeit and pirated products in the UK amounted to almost GBP 100 million in 2013.
- **Impacts on jobs**: Global counterfeiting and piracy in 2013 resulted in 60 000 lost jobs in the UK, comprising 40 000 in the retail and wholesale sector, and 20 000 in the manufacturing sector. This represents 1.15% of all employees in the UK.

- **Impacts on government revenue**: Counterfeit trade meant the UK government lost almost GBP 3.8 billion in tax revenue, of which GBP 2.4 billion were due to counterfeit imports to the UK and 1.4 billion were due to illicit trade in goods that infringe IPR of UK residents. This represents around 1% of the taxes the UK government should have collected on corporate profits, personal incomes, consumption (VAT) and social security contributions.

These estimated losses refer to direct economic impacts only; long-term effects (e.g. on innovation) and other effects (e.g. health and safety) are not included due to data limitations. If added, the total effect of counterfeiting and piracy on the UK economy would be much higher.

The findings should help both public and private sector decision makers to better understand the nature and scale of the trade in counterfeit goods for the UK economy, and to develop appropriate, cohesive, and evidence-based policy responses.

Chapter 1.

Quantifying the UK impacts of the global trade in counterfeit products: methodological background

The entire UK economy relies on some form of intellectual property (IP), because virtually every industry either produces or uses it. The flipside of the value of IP is the harm caused by IP theft, involving creating and selling counterfeit and pirated products. Information on the magnitude, scope and trends of counterfeit and pirated trade is critical to understand the nature of the problem and how the situation is evolving. It is also essential for designing and implementing effective policies and measures to combat illicit operations. This report describes an analysis conducted by the OECD of the economic impact on the UK economy of the global trade in counterfeit and pirated goods. This chapter takes a step-by-step approach to explain the unique methodology used for the analysis.

Introduction

Industries relying intensively on intellectual property (IP) play a significant role in the economy of the United Kingdom (UK), and serve as a primary driver of UK economic growth and national competitiveness. These important industries rely on the recognition and effective enforcement of a variety of intangible assets and products of the mind and human intellect, which we refer to collectively as "intellectual property."

The story of IP is a story of economic growth, high-paying jobs, economic competitiveness, innovation and creative expression. The entire UK economy relies on some form of IP, because virtually every industry either produces or uses it. In addition to being a major driver of UK economic growth, IP provides the incentive to create, invest in, and commercialize new inventions, products, and services, while supporting artists and authors in disseminating their works, be it literary, artistic, musical, cinematic, or other creative forms of human expression.

Alongside this remarkably positive story of economic growth, ingenuity and creativity lies the less positive story of IP theft and the harm it does. It is essential to understanding these threats and the impediments to effective IP enforcement at the macro-level—that is, their global scope and magnitude—and at the micro level—the nature of the complex schemes used by illicit actors to accomplish IP theft on a commercial scale. Without it, developing and implementing an effective strategy to tackle it would be impossible.

Information on the magnitude, scope and trends of counterfeit and pirated trade is critical to understand the nature of the problem and how the situation is evolving. Information is also essential for designing and implementing effective policies and measures to combat illicit operations. This report describes an analysis conducted by the OECD of the economic impact on the UK economy of the global trade in counterfeit and pirated goods. This chapter outlines the general methodology developed through a step-by-step approach. Chapter 2 presents the findings of the methodology applied to the UK. Chapter 3 reviews the next steps needed to improve the evidence base for future studies. Chapter 4 concludes with a round-up of the policy-relevant findings.

Where do data on counterfeit and pirated trade come from?

Precise quantification and measurement of the global reach and economic scale of counterfeiting and commercial piracy, and the losses attributable to trade secret theft, can prove elusive. This is because counterfeiting and commercial-scale piracy are illicit activities, making data on such activities and their impact inherently difficult to obtain.

The clandestine and illicit nature of counterfeiting and piracy imply that the available data falls far short of what is needed for robust analysis and policy making (Box 1.1). It means that the statistical information on the magnitude, scope and trends of counterfeit and pirated trade becomes the critical component in the design process of any methodology that sheds some light on this phenomenon. Put differently, the starting point for any quantitative analysis in the area of counterfeit trade is to verify what sort of statistical data are available for analysing this issue.

This report required three types of data, each discussed in the sections which follow:

- data on counterfeit and pirated trade
- international trade statistics
- other data, including on consumer behaviour regarding counterfeit and pirated fakes, and other background micro and macroeconomic data.

Box 1.1. Data limitations

It is important to highlight that the data on counterfeiting and piracy are scarce and incomplete. Even though some progress in data collection has been observed over recent years, available statistics on counterfeiting and piracy still need significant improvement. Consequently, there are three things that should be kept in mind when developing and applying a methodological framework to quantify the effects of counterfeit trade.

1. The framework developed here does not claim to quantify all the impacts of counterfeit and pirated trade on the UK economy. It looks at areas where quantification was possible, while identifying areas of work needed to improve the understanding of how counterfeit and pirated trade affects economies and societies overall.

Box 1.1. Data limitations *(continued)*

2. In areas where quantification was possible, the framework relies on a set of methodological assumptions. For transparency purposes all are clearly spelt out in the text.
3. The framework leaves scope for further methodological amendments subject to future data improvements. There are several areas where improvements could be done, for example gauging consumers' rates of substitutions between fake and genuine goods (Chapter 3).

Data on counterfeit and pirated trade

The best available information on counterfeit and pirated trade comes from the OECD database on customs seizures. This was constructed by combining three separate datasets, received from the World Customs Organisation (WCO), the Directorate-General for Taxation and Customs Union (DG TAXUD) of the European Commission, and the US Department of Homeland Security. The database includes detailed information on seizures of IPR-infringing goods made by customs officers in 99 economies around the world between 2010 and 2013. For each year, there are more than 100 000 observations entered into the database (in most cases one observation corresponds to one customs seizure). These statistics were used in a large-scale assessment by the OECD and European Union Intellectual Property Office (EUIPO), which revised the global estimate of international trade in counterfeit and pirated goods (OECD-EUIPO, 2016).

The database contains a wealth of information about IPR-infringing goods and can be used for detailed quantitative and qualitative analysis. In most cases, the database reports general information, such as the date of seizure, the provenance and destination economies, the conveyance method, the product category, as well as more detailed descriptions, such as the name of legitimate brand owner, the number of seized products and their approximate value.

Importantly, the three original customs datasets rely on data entries collected and processed by customs officers. These data are primarily designed to improve the work of customs, e.g. to prepare risk profiling processes and share national experiences. As with any other administrative data they need careful consideration before use in quantitative analysis. A detailed analysis of the data revealed a set of limitations with this dataset, including inconsistencies in product classification levels, anomalies in terms of seized goods' provenance economies and valuations. All these issues were addressed in OECD-EUIPO (2016).

Concerning valuation of seized goods, it should be recalled that structured interviews with customs officials and descriptive analysis of values of selected products conducted as part of the OECD-EUIPO project revealed that the declared values are reported in most cases. The issue of valuation of seized goods is discussed in more detail in Chapter 3 of this report.

Trade statistics

The trade statistics used in this report are based on the United Nations (UN) Comtrade database. With 171 reporting economies which report data, and 247 partner economies (76 economies in addition to reporting economies), the database is considered the most comprehensive trade database available. Products are registered on a six-digit Harmonized System (HS)[1] basis, meaning that the level of detail is high. Data used in this study are based on landed customs value, which is the value of merchandise assigned by customs officials. In most instances this is the same as the transaction value appearing on accompanying invoices. Landed customs value includes the insurance and freight charges incurred when transporting goods from the economy of origin to the economy of importation.

In most economies, import statistics are compiled from the records filed with local customs authorities. This is particularly important in the context of this report as all datasets used in the statistical exercise (trade statistics and data on customs seizures of infringing products) originate from the same source – customs offices at the destination.

Other data

Other statistical information was used to develop a methodology to gauge the economic impact of trade in fake goods. These include:

- Statistical information on sectoral production, sales, jobs, and wages, extracted from national statistics offices.
- Information on consumers' substitution rates (see below) between genuine goods and fake goods contained in various academic studies and consumers surveys.

A more detailed discussion of these datasets is presented later in this chapter.

How to measure the economic impact of trade in counterfeit products?

There are two ways in which counterfeit products affect the UK (Figure 1.1):

1. the effects of imports of counterfeit and pirated products on consumers, industries (including manufacturing, wholesale and retail) and government.
2. the effects of infringements of intellectual property rights (IPRs) on right holders and government.

Three important things should be kept in mind when analysing these impacts. Firstly, the methodology refers to the notion of ***primary*** and ***secondary markets*** for counterfeit and pirated goods, i.e. it distinguishes between fake products that *deceive* consumers (primary markets) and those that are *openly sold* as fakes to consumers (secondary markets: see OECD-EUIPO, 2016). The markets for deceptive and non-deceptive products have significantly different characteristics, and these differences have important implications for the overall assessment.

Whereas in primary markets consumers pay the full (or approximately) retail price for a fake product thinking that it is genuine, consumers knowingly purchasing IPR-infringing products in secondary markets are likely to pay a lower price, and would have not necessarily substituted the fakes for the genuine goods given the choice. Obviously, these differences in price and substitution rates have different implications for the estimation of lost sales and lost taxes, and for the valuation of consumers' detriment (the price premium unjustly paid by consumers in the belief that they are buying a genuine product).

Figure 1.1. How counterfeit and pirated trade affects industries, government and consumers

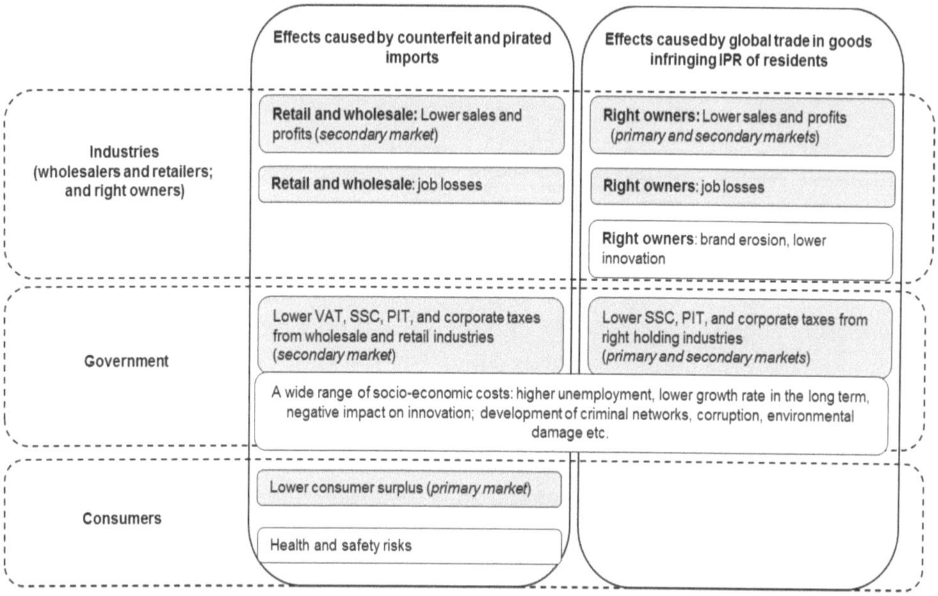

Notes:

1. Grey indicates areas for which quantitative analysis of impact is possible (with different degree of robustness of final results). White indicates areas for which quantitative analysis of impact is currently not possible.
2. VAT refers to value-added taxes, SSC to social security contributions, PIT to personal income taxes.

Other impact areas are hard to measure quantitatively, or are likely to occur in the long term, and are therefore excluded from the analysis. These include, for example, the negative effects of counterfeiting and piracy on consumer health and safety, on the environment, on the proliferation of criminal networks or on long-term innovation and growth.

Who is affected and how?

Industry

There are numerous industry groups that are affected badly by global counterfeiting and piracy. Legitimate wholesalers and retailers record lower sales because customers sometimes prefer to buy a fake product. Legitimate IP right holders suffer from lower revenues and profits, and in the long term they face significant brand erosion, because of unfair competition from counterfeiters that free ride on their IP (see Box 1.2).

On the other hand, some industries can actually benefit from counterfeiting and piracy. In countries producing fake goods, counterfeiting generates significant economic activity that could be beneficial for many industry players. In addition some intermediaries, such as express and shipping companies, may record higher demand for their services because of counterfeit trade.

This methodology focuses only on *losses* incurred by the industry due to counterfeiting and piracy, and does not take into account either the positive impact of production of counterfeit products, or potential gains that intermediaries derive from counterfeit trade. There are two main reasons for this. Firstly, there are not enough data to determine precisely the potentially positive impact on producers and intermediaries. Too little is still known about the exact nature of counterfeit operations to establish a sound econometric framework that could quantify it. Secondly, parties that gain from counterfeiting and piracy often operate in an illegal economic environment. Hence, the benefits they derive do not contribute to social welfare, and result in a set of negative externalities, such as erosion of the legal system, corruption of governance structures and emergence of criminal networks.

Consequently, this methodology looks at two industry groups in the UK specifically affected by counterfeiting and piracy: (1) wholesale and retail businesses; and (2) right owners.

The wholesale and retail sector is affected by the sale of fake products on secondary markets, i.e. by consumers who intentionally buy fake products. This is because their sale implies lower legitimate sales for retailers, and consequently, lower profits and less jobs.

IP rights holders are affected by world trade in those counterfeit and pirated products that infringe their rights. In the short term, such trade reduces sales volumes and hence lowers profits made by the right holders. These losses happen due to sales of counterfeit and pirated products on both primary and secondary markets. However, each market has a different rate of sales displacement. Finally, lower sales and profits might also lead to lower levels of employment.

Government

For governments, the principal effects of counterfeit and pirated trade are foregone tax revenues. Firstly, lower sales volume and profits made by rights holders, wholesalers and retailers directly reduce corporate income taxes. Secondly, sales on secondary markets are not likely to be registered, resulting in reduced sales taxes and value-added taxes on sales made by wholesalers and retailers. Finally, job losses induced by counterfeiting reduce payroll taxes, social security contributions, and personal income taxes.

In the longer term, counterfeit trade can also have some broader, more general socio-economic effects for governments, including effects on trade, innovation and growth, employment, the environment, and criminal activity. However, due to lack of sufficient and consistent cross-economy statistics, quantification of these impacts is not possible at this stage (see Box 1.2).

Box 1.2. The long-term effects of counterfeiting and piracy

Counterfeit and pirated products can have profound long-term implications. For industries, the continued presence of counterfeit products may damage the value of the brand and image of the producers of genuine products. For instance, consumers who purchase fake items in the belief that they are genuine will be likely to blame the manufacturer of the genuine product if the fake does not fulfil expectations, thus damaging goodwill. If consumers never discover that they have been deceived, they may be reluctant to buy another product from that manufacturer, and may communicate the information to other potential buyers. Also consumers who purchase the genuine article may be put off by the availability of counterfeited products. Given that consumers are aware of potential deception on the primary market, they could adjust their expectation about future consumption patterns.

In addition, lower revenues and profits induced by counterfeiting and piracy lead in turn to lower investments by rights holders, including investments in research and development (R&D). This could translate into less innovation, slowing technical progress and lowering the rate of economic growth in the longer term.

These long-term effects cannot be quantified for two main reasons. Firstly, to do so would generally require data spanning several years. Such data are unavailable. Secondly, existing studies that could contribute to producing an adequate, alternative methodology are mostly theoretical and do not provide robust empirical support.

Consumers

For consumers, counterfeit and pirated trade might reduce the value or satisfaction that they derive from the concerned products. This is based in large measure on differences in product quality and/or performance for similarly-priced products. This is likely to occur, for instance, when a consumer buys a low-quality fake product on the primary market, believing it to be a high-quality genuine good.

In addition, counterfeit and pirated trade dramatically increases the potential for negative effects on the health and safety of consumers. Counterfeiters who target the primary market while seeking to maximise profits have limited or no interest in ensuring the quality, efficacy or safety of their products (Box 1.3.). However, because data are not collected systematically, most evidence on negative health and safety effects is anecdotal; more work is needed to measure the effects more broadly.

Box 1.3. Health risks and counterfeit hair straighteners

Hair straighteners are very commonly counterfeited, with a number of premium brands regularly being faked. A genuine version of these usually retails at around GBP 90-100, whilst the counterfeit can be purchased from a market stall for approximately GBP 30. However, counterfeits have been sold online for around GBP 70, which may seem to close enough to the real price to suggest to consumers that the product is genuine, but offered at a discount.

A detailed examination of a sample of fake hair straighteners done by Electrical Safety First showed that the internal components of fake products were compromised and severely lacking in both function and basic essential safety features. In addition, unlike the genuine product, the fake product did not have any additional safety features, such as an automatic cut-off which turns off the heating plates after a given amount of time to reduce the risk of fire and burns to the user.

Source: Electrical Safety First (2016), "A shocking rip off: The true cost of counterfeit electrical products", http://www.electricalsafetyfirst.org.uk/mediafile/100492991/True-Cost-of-a-Counterfeit.pdf.

To summarise, there are seven impact areas that this study is able to quantify with a relatively high degree of robustness. Four of them are the impacts of imports of fake goods on a specific economy: (1) loss of sales, (2) job losses, (3) lower tax revenues, and (4) loss of consumer welfare. The three remaining areas are impacts caused by global trade in products that infringe the IPR of the economy's residents. These include: (5) lower sales for the industry, (6) job losses, and (7) lower tax revenues.

The methodological framework developed to calculate all these effects is presented step by step in the subsections below. Note that this methodology takes into account the "double-counting" issue which arises from the existence of imports of fake products in the UK economy that infringe the IPRs of its own residents.

How to quantify the direct effects of imports of fake products?

The first four impact areas listed above, can be calculated from the database on worldwide customs seizures of IPR-infringing products. The methodology follows a number of steps:

1. Estimating the value of imports of counterfeit and pirated products.
2. Estimating the value of fake imported products sold in the primary and secondary markets.
3. Estimating consumer detriment.
4. Estimating lost sales for retailers and wholesalers.
5. Estimating job losses in the retail and wholesale sector.
6. Estimating taxes foregone.

Figure 1.2. Steps involved in analysing the economic effects of counterfeit and pirated imports

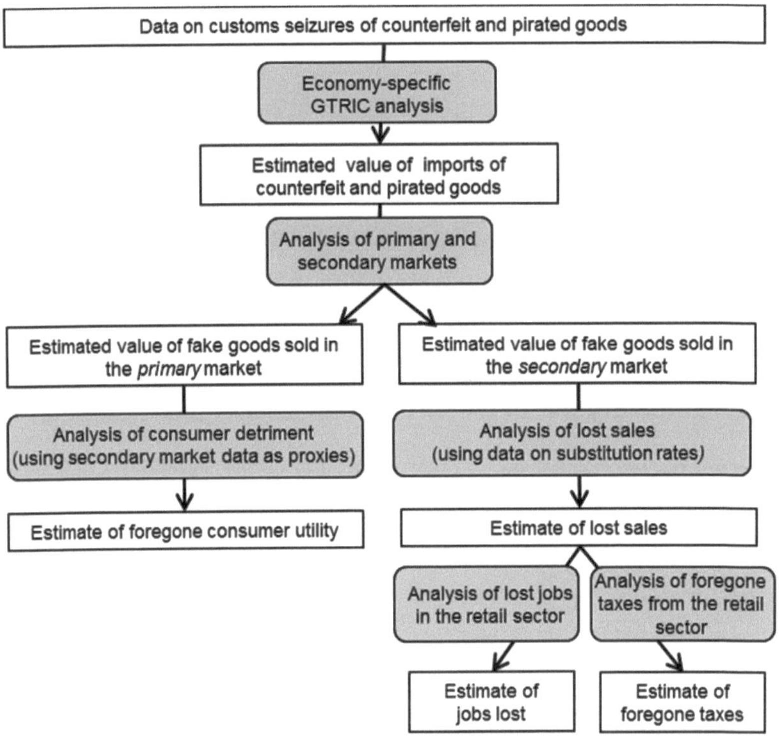

Step 1: Estimating the value of imports of counterfeit and pirated products

This first step involved tailoring the databases on customs seizures of IP-infringing products and on imports of genuine goods to estimate the import value of counterfeit and pirated goods by product category and provenance economy. This partial dataset then formed the basis for further analysis of impacts.

The first task was to select out of the general database on customs seizures of IP-infringing goods observations that refer to the UK as "destination economy". The second task was to apply the General Trade-Related Index of Counterfeiting (GTRIC) methodology to this data selection in order to gauge the value of fake imports for each product category and provenance economy identified. The GTRIC methodology allows the economy-specific trade context to be taken into account, and relies on two key econometric components (see Annex A and OECD-EUIPO, 2016 for more detail):

- The GTRIC indices for economies (GTRIC-e) and for products (GTRIC-p). GTRIC-e is an index which ranks economies according to their relative propensity to be an economy of provenance for counterfeit products. GTRIC-p is an index of industries according to their relative propensity to be targeted for counterfeiting.
- The GTRIC matrix, obtained by combining GTRIC-e and GTRIC-p. This matrix assigns the relative probability that a given type of product imported from a given trading partner will be counterfeit or pirated compared to the most sensitive to counterfeiting "product category-provenance economy" pair.

Importantly, two assumptions are made to calculate the GTRIC vectors. The first one is that the volume of seizures of a given product or from a given source economy is positively correlated with the actual intensity of trade in counterfeit and pirated goods in this product category or from that economy. The second assumption acknowledges that this relationship is not linear, as there might be some biases in the detection and seizure procedures. For instance, the fact that infringing goods are detected more frequently in certain categories could imply that differences in counterfeiting factors across products merely reflect that some goods are easier to detect than others, or that some goods, for one reason or another, have been specially targeted for inspection.

While the GTRIC matrix does not provide a direct measure of the overall magnitude of counterfeit and pirated imports, it establishes statistical relationships that are useful for this purpose. More specifically, applying the GTRIC matrix to statistics on imports of genuine products allows the upper limit value for imports in counterfeit and pirated goods to be gauged.

Similar to OECD-EUIPO (2016), this approach is taken by establishing an upper limit of counterfeit trade (in percentages of the economy's imports) for the key "provenance economy-product category" pairs that are the most vulnerable to counterfeiting, i.e. with the highest relative likelihood of being counterfeit or pirated.

Following OECD-EUIPO (2016), these values are called “fixed points”.

In their main report on counterfeit trade, the OECD and EUIPO (2016) gauged the fixed point for a range of six “industry-provenance” pairs where shares of counterfeit products are the highest, based on a focus group meeting and on interviews with customs officials. The results were refined using a set of supplementary data on seizures in dedicated actions provided by the European Anti-Fraud Office (OLAF).

Once established, “the fixed points” combined with the relative probabilities included in GTRIC matrix allow the share of fake imports contained in every “product category-provenance economy” pair to be determined. These shares are then applied to existing statistics on trade in genuine products to estimate the total value of counterfeit and pirated imports.

Step 2: Estimating the value of fake goods sold in the primary and secondary markets

Two questions are crucial in assessing the economic impact of counterfeit and pirated imports for domestic retail and wholesale industries, consumers, and the government. First, what is the proportion of counterfeit and pirated imports that are sold on primary versus secondary markets? Second, within secondary markets, what is the rate at which UK consumers are substituting counterfeit goods for legitimate products?

The distinction between primary and secondary markets described earlier is crucial for analysing the effects of counterfeit and pirated imports on an economy. Every sale of a fake good on a primary market clearly represents a direct loss for the retail and wholesale industry. In secondary markets, however, only a share of consumers would have deliberately substituted their purchases of counterfeit products for legitimate ones, because in secondary markets they know what they are buying is fake. The key issue is then how to calculate the consumers’ substitution rate, i.e. the extent to which every illegal purchase displaces a legal sale.

Estimating the share of fakes sold on primary and secondary markets

In order to distinguish fake products that counterfeiters and pirates intended to sell on the primary market from those intended for sale on the secondary market, the price gap between both types of fakes is exploited. For each case of custom seizure specified in the database, customs authorities report the declared value of goods (see Box 1.4. Valuation of fake goods: declared and replacement values), the quantity seized, the product's HS code, and the infringed trademark. This allows the unit value of each seized "product type-brand" pair[2] to be calculated. These unit values can then serve as a proxy for the retail prices of the fake goods.

Box 1.4. Valuation of fake goods: declared and replacement values

In general, there are two principles followed by customs officials when reporting the value of counterfeit and pirated goods: 1) declared value (value indicated on customs declarations), which corresponds to values reported in the general trade statistics; and 2) replacement value (price of original goods). However, it is often unclear ex ante whether the reported value relates to transaction or replacement. The structured interviews with customs officials and the descriptive analysis of values of selected products conducted in OECD/EUIPO (2016) reveal that the declared values are reported for most cases.

Thus, for each type of product associated with a given trademark or patent, the prices of seized goods are used to estimate a confidence interval that contains the actual retail price of the corresponding genuine item. Counterfeit and pirated items whose unit price, calculated as described above, are higher than or included in this interval are then classified as intended for sale on the primary market. Those whose price is below this interval are classified as targeting the secondary market.[3]

For example, Figure 1.3 shows the price distribution of fake UGG boots produced by the American brand Deckers Outdoor Corporation that were seized by UK customs between 2011 and 2013. Using the methodology outlined indicates that fakes with prices lower than GBP 165 were destined for the secondary market, while those with values higher than GBP 165 pounds (the peak on the right hand side of the distribution) were targeted at the primary market. For more examples, see Annex A.3.

Figure 1.3. Price distribution of fake UGG boots seized worldwide, 2011-2013

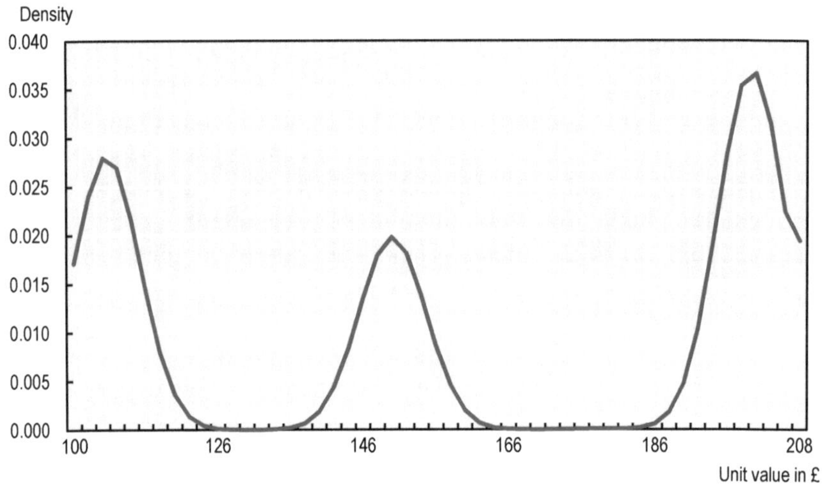

Substitution rates on secondary markets

In primary markets, consumers pay the full retail price for a fake product thinking that it is the genuine good. The assumption can be made that a legitimate item would have been bought in the absence of the fake product. This represents a one-to-one substitution rate (a 100% displacement rate) and thus, a one-to-one direct loss for the industry. Note that this one-to-one substitution rate requires three important conditions: (1) the consumer is paying full retail price (or near enough) for the fake product; (2) the consumer is not aware he/she is purchasing a counterfeit product; and (3) the fake good is almost identical in quality to the genuine one.

In secondary markets, consumers knowingly purchase IP infringing products (Box 1.5.). The issue is then to estimate the likelihood that consumers would have purchased the genuine product at its full price. Clearly, these substitution rates vary by industry and economy, since factors such as product quality, distribution channels, and information available about the product can differ significantly. They also depend on the consumer's motives for purchasing counterfeit and pirated goods. For example some consumers buy counterfeits for fun, which may not provide any guidance on specific values to use.

As mentioned previously, the substitution rate is the assumed rate at which a consumer is willing to switch from purchasing a fake good to the genuine product. In other words, this displacement analysis seeks to identify the extent to which consumers substitute purchases of counterfeit and pirated products for legitimate ones. The main goal is to identify sales that were never realised by industries due to counterfeiting and piracy. Formally, a displacement rate of $x\%$ means that every $100/x$ illegal purchases of a given counterfeit product displace a legal sale.

Box 1.5. Why do people buy fakes knowingly?

There are numerous reasons identified in the scientific literature for why people buy fakes. Firstly, if the genuine product is hard to get hold of, this greatly influences the perception of its value. Furthermore, the willingness of consumers to purchase a counterfeit product seems to increase if they can rate the quality of a product before purchase and to decrease if they cannot. The situation surrounding the purchase also determines purchase intentions. The situational mood explains why some people are more prone to buy counterfeits even if that this is illegal or the lack of post-purchase satisfaction with a product of low quality. Recent psychological research illustrates a number of other motivations, such as the "thrill of the hunt," being part of a "secret society" and genuine interest. Buyers of counterfeit products also try to legitimise their behavior and give reasons for justifications.

Sources: Bian, et al., (2016), "New insights into unethical counterfeit consumption", *Journal of Business Research,* 69(10): 4249-4258; Bian, X., Haque, S. and Smith, A. (2015), "Social power, product conspicuousness and the demand for luxury brand counterfeit products", *British Journal of Social Psychology*, 54(1): 37-54; Eisend, M. and Schuchert-Güler, P. (2006), "Explaining counterfeit purchases, a review and preview", *Academy of Marketing Science Review*, 12: 1–25.

Information on substitution rates can be obtained from two different sources: academic research on consumers' social-economic behaviour, and consumer surveys. The majority of academic research has however focused on intangible pirated products, such as digital piracy.[4] Findings are rarer for tangible products, with the exception of luxury products. For example, Yoo and Lee (2005) studied the behaviour of Korean female college students and found a substitution rate of 21% for luxury fashion clothing and accessories.

In another study consumers were presented with an opportunity to purchase counterfeit products in a simulated shopping experience (Tom et al., 1998). When given the choice between a counterfeit or legitimate version of the product, 32% of the consumers selected the counterfeit version and 68% opted for the legitimate version.[56] The preference for counterfeit or legitimate versions differs by product category. Counterfeit t-shirts were the most popular (42% stated a preference for the counterfeit version), while counterfeit software was the least popular (17% stated a preference for the fake software).

The issue of the variability of substitution rates between product categories has been barely addressed in consumer surveys. One of the exceptions is a survey conducted by the Anti-Counterfeiting Group (2007), in which a sample of 1 003 representative UK consumers aged 16 and over were asked if they would have bought anything had the fake item not been available. Among this sample, 39% of consumers responded that they would have bought a genuine alternative (either made by the brand or another brand) in the case of clothing or footwear products, 49% in the case of fragrance, and 27% in the case of watches.[7]

Given the scarcity of data, the empirical exercise performed in Chapter 2 relies on three different scenarios. The first scenario assumes substitution rates that follow the results of the Anti-Counterfeiting Group's (2007) consumer survey. In this scenario, a substitution rate of 39% has been chosen for product category related to clothing and footwear, meaning that every GBP 2.5 spent on fake clothes, accessories or footwear in secondary markets translate into GBP 1 in lost sales for the retail and wholesale industry. Also in accordance with this consumer survey, the selected rates in scenario 1 are 49% for products related to the perfumery and cosmetics sector, and 27% for products belonging to the watch and jewellery industries. Finally, according to the study carried out by Tom et al. (1998), the selected substitution rate is 32% for all other fake products sold on secondary markets. The second scenario is more conservative, and assumes substitution rates 10 percentage points lower. The third scenario is the most conservative one, and assumes the substitution rates to be 20 percentage points lower than in the first scenario.

In order to test the robustness of the results, the estimates of lost sales, lost jobs and lost taxes will rely on three alternative scenarios based on lower assumed consumers' substitution rates. These are presented in Table 1.1below.

Table 1.1 Assumed consumers' substitution rates in the three performed scenarios

Sector	Scenario 1	Scenario 2	Scenario 3
Perfumery and cosmetics	49%	39%	29%
Watches and jewellery	27%	17%	7%
Clothing, accessories, leather and related products	39%	29%	19%
Other sectors	32%	22%	12%

Step 3: Estimating consumer detriment

An individual consumer detriment is the price premium unjustly paid by the consumer in the belief that they are buying a genuine product. As consumers who choose to purchase counterfeit products on secondary markets deliberately make a cost-quality trade-off, consumer detriment only occurs in primary markets. For each product category the individual consumer detriment is estimated by calculating the difference between average price paid in the primary market (by deceived consumers) and in the secondary market (by consumers who knowingly buy fake goods). This individual consumer detriment is then multiplied by the total volume of transactions in the primary market in a given product category. Finally, for all product categories the detriments are added together to give a general estimate of consumer detriment.[8]

Step 4: Estimating lost sales for retailers and wholesalers

In order to measure lost sales for retailers and wholesalers due to counterfeit imports, three sets of information are used:

1. The estimated value of counterfeit imports by industry, as obtained in Step 1.
2. The shares of primary and secondary markets, which are estimated at the most detailed level (ideally, by brand and product type) using the methodology described in the first part of Step 2.
3. Information on consumers' substitution rates, which are extracted from consumer surveys, as explained in the second part of Step 2.

The estimated value of counterfeit imports combined with the share of the primary market gives us the total volume of lost sales for retailers and wholesalers due to the unsuspecting purchase of counterfeit products. The estimated value of counterfeit imports, combined with the shares of the secondary market and consumers' substitution rates gives us the total volume of lost sales for retailers and wholesalers due to the knowing purchase of counterfeit products. This takes into account the fact that those consumers would not have necessarily bought the genuine alternatives if the fakes had not been available.[9] Finally, the sum of both estimates gives us the total value of lost sales for wholesalers and retailers due to counterfeit imports.

Step 5: Estimating jobs lost in the retail and wholesale sector

The economic literature does not make clear links between the values of lost sales and lost jobs for each industry. This study therefore developed a simple econometric model to address this issue (see Annex A.3 for an in-depth description). The aim is to explain the extent to which the retail and wholesale industry adjusts their employment when their sales vary.

This econometric exercise was first implemented for the UK retail and wholesale industries (Table A.1 Annex A). The main insight at the aggregate level is that an increase in 1% of sales in the retail and wholesale sector implies on average a 0.46% increase in the number of employees within the sector.

The estimates of the sales elasticity of employment for each category of the UK retail and wholesale industry are reported in Table 1.2. Clearly, a decrease in sales is not translated into the same proportion of lost jobs in each sector. For instance, while a decline of 1% in sales for the wholesale and retail sector of chemical products induce a 0.37% decline in the number of employees within this sector, the elasticity is far higher for the wholesale and retail sector of clothing, accessories and footwear, with an estimated transmission rate of 0.58%.

Table 1.2. Elasticity of employment with respect to sales for the UK wholesale and retail sector, 2011-2013

Sector	Sales elasticity of employment*
Food, beverages and tobacco	0.53
Mineral products (e.g. fuels, ores)	0.45
Chemical and allied products;	0.37
Pharmaceutical and medicinal chemical products	0.45
Perfumery and cosmetics	0.45
Textiles and other intermediate products	0.51
Clothing, footwear, leather and related products	0.58
Watches and jewellery	0.44
Non-metallic mineral products	0.48
Basic metals and fabricated metal products	0.48
Electrical household appliances, electronics and telecommunications	0.49
Machinery; computers and peripheral equipment; ships and aircrafts	0.52
Motor vehicles and motorcycles	0.57
Household cultural and recreation goods;	0.53
Furniture, lighting equipment, carpets and other manufacturing n.e.c	0.58

Once estimated, these transmission rates between sales and jobs can be used to estimate the share of lost jobs due to counterfeit imports in total employment. For each retail and wholesale industry, this is done by multiplying the transmission rate with the share of lost sales into the total sales of genuine products. Finally, applying these shares of lost jobs onto data on the level of employment in a given sector allows us to estimate the number of jobs lost in the wholesale and retail industries due to counterfeit imports.[10]

Step 6: Determining taxes foregone

Lower genuine sales due to counterfeit and pirated imports reduce several sources of revenue for government:

- value-added taxes (VAT) that would have been collected on consumption
- corporate income taxes (CIT) that would have been collected on firms in the wholesale and retail industries

- social security contributions (SSC) for employees and employers in the retail and wholesale industries
- personal income taxes (PIT) for employees and employers in the retail and wholesale industries.

In order to calculate the lost VAT, one simply needs to apply the VAT rate on the amount of total lost sales due to counterfeit and pirated imports estimated in Step 4. The amount of government taxes lost from CIT is calculated by multiplying the average profit rates within each category of retail and wholesale industry with the average rate of corporation tax and the estimated value of lost sales.

To calculate losses in social security contributions, the share of the actual average amount of SSC paid by employees and employers for one unit of employment is multiplied by the amount of estimated lost jobs due to counterfeit and pirated imports estimated in Step 5. The PIT foregone is calculated by multiplying the average salary in a given industry by the average income tax rate times the amount of lost jobs.

Note that in order to estimate the results as accurately as possible, these four types of lost revenues were calculated by industry. The final result at the national level was obtained by summing the estimated amounts of foregone tax revenues across industries.

Box 1.6. The OECD BEPS programme

The OECD base erosion and profit shifting (BEPS) programme tackles tax avoidance strategies that exploit gaps and mismatches in tax rules to artificially shift profits to low or no-tax locations. Although some of the schemes used are illegal, most are not. However, the practice undermines the fairness and integrity of tax systems because businesses that operate across borders can use BEPS to gain a competitive advantage over enterprises that operate at a domestic level. Moreover, when taxpayers see multinational corporations legally avoiding income tax, it undermines voluntary compliance by all taxpayers.

Under the BEPS framework, over 100 economies collaborate to implement measures to counter tax planning strategies that exploit these gaps and mismatches. The Inclusive Framework on BEPS has released information on the domestic legal frameworks for country-by-country (CbC) reporting around the world. This provides a high-level snapshot for tax administrations on currently implemented measures to counter such tax planning strategies.

Finally, one should keep in mind that the degree of tax losses also depends on the efficiency of tax collection schemes. An inefficient fiscal system might allow companies to exploit gaps and mismatches in tax rules to artificially shift profits to low or no-tax locations where there is little or no economic activity. The OECD base erosion and profit shifting programme (BEPS) was designed to tackle this problem (Box 1.6.). According to its recent findings referring to the country-by-country reporting, the UK is one of the countries with the most advanced legislative framework to counter this problem.

How to gauge the direct effects of trade in fake goods on UK IP right holders?

There are three ways global trade in counterfeit and pirated products can affect IP right holders: (1) loss of sales, (2) job losses, and (3) foregone tax revenues. These can be calculated using a harmonised methodology that is very close to the previous analysis.

Figure 1.4. Analysis of the impacts on IP right holders of global trade in fakes

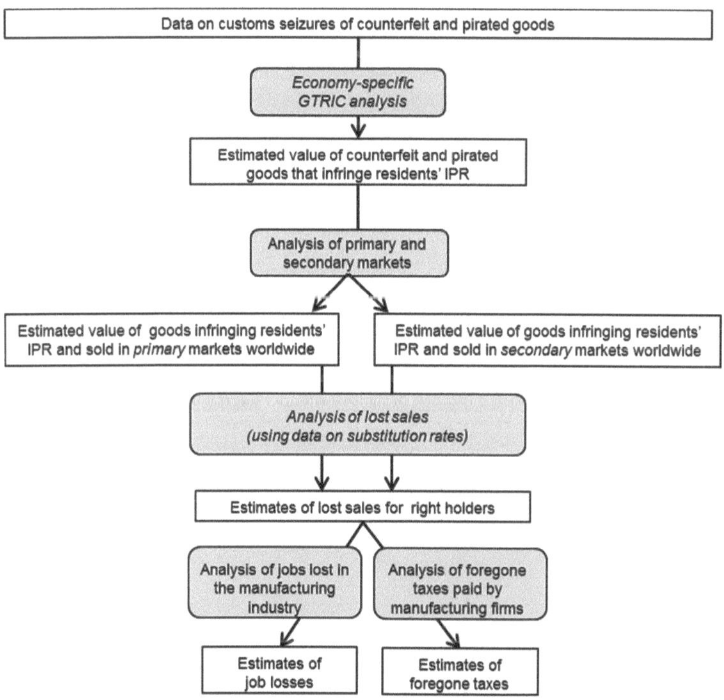

Just as for the analysis of the effects of fake imports, this analysis draws on the database on worldwide seizures of IPR-infringing products. The methodology follows a number of steps:

- Step 7: Evaluating the worldwide volume of infringement of UK IPR rights holders.
- Step 8: Market analysis of residents' IPR infringing goods sold worldwide (primary/secondary).
- Step 9: Analysis of lost sales for IP right holders.
- Step 10: Estimation of lost jobs for manufacturing industries.
- Step 11: Estimation of foregone taxes.

Step 7: Evaluating the worldwide volume of infringements of IPRs of UK right holders

The first step is to estimate the value of counterfeit goods traded worldwide that infringe trademarks or patents held by UK right owners. For this purpose, observations in the database that refer to trademarks or patents whose right holders' address is registered in the UK were selected. Note that the identification of right holders' location was done using the Global Brand Database (WIPO, 2016a) and the PATENTSCOPE database (WIPO, 2016b), both provided by the World Intellectual Property Organisation. The former gathers around 30 million records of brand registration from 35 national and international collections worldwide, while the latter provides access to more than 59 million patent documents of participating national and regional patent offices.

In total more than 60% of seizures data were able to be matched with the right holder information. From this data selection, the value of global counterfeiting targeting the IPRs of UK residents can be assessed by product category and destination economy, by adapting the GTRIC methodology for exports and domestic sales.

This time, the propensities included in the GTRIC matrix refer to the likelihood that a counterfeit product of a brand or patent whose right holders' location is registered in the UK is exported to a given destination. These propensities are then applied to existing statistics on exports and domestic sales to estimate the overall magnitude of global trade in counterfeit and pirated products that infringe UK residents' IPRs.

This methodology allows the general exporting and selling behaviour of industries to be taken into account, and relies on three key econometric components:

- The General Trade-Related Index of Counterfeiting for economies (GTRIC-e): an index which lists economies according to their propensity to be a destination for counterfeit and pirated products of brands registered in the UK.
- The General Trade-Related Index of Counterfeiting for ICT products (GTRIC-p): an index which lists industries according to their propensity to sell products that are sensitive to global counterfeiting and piracy.
- The General Trade-Related Index of Counterfeiting matrix (GTRIC) that compares the likelihood of products sold by a given industry in a given destination economy to be counterfeit or pirated with the most sensitive "product category-destination economy" pair.

Again, applying the GTRIC matrix to data on exports and domestic sales allows the "ceiling" value to be gauged for trade in counterfeit and pirated goods infringing the IPR owned by UK residents. One issue, however, is how to establish a "fixed point", i.e. an upper limit of counterfeit trade, in percentage of exports, for the "product category–destination economy" pairs that are the most sensitive to global counterfeiting and piracy.

Since the interviews with customs officials and experts could not determine these "fixed points", the empirical application is based on three scenarios, with selected values of 10%, 15% and 20%. Note that all of these scenarios take much more conservative values of "fixed points" than the actual "fixed points" applied for imports in OECD-EUIPO (2016).

These "fixed points", when combined with the relative likelihood included in the GTRIC matrix allow us to calculate the share of exports and, importantly, of domestic sales of products infringing residents' IPRs. Applying these shares to statistics on the value of exports and domestic sales gives the estimated value of goods infringing residents' IPR by product category and destination economy.

Step 8: Market analysis of fake goods infringing the UK's IPRs

As with the previous analysis, two issues need now to be addressed in order to assess the economic impact of infringements of domestic right owners' trademarks and patents in global trade. First, what share of these counterfeit products is traded on primary versus secondary markets worldwide? Second, within secondary markets, what is the rate at which consumers across the world would have substituted counterfeit goods for their legitimate copies?

The first issue is addressed with the exact same methodology as described in the first part of Step 2. The only slight difference is that the unit value distributions are estimated for each "product category-trademark (or patent)-destination economy" triplet, in order to take into account differences in retail prices between economies. Finally, because of a lack of data, the consumers' substitution rates chosen are the same as those selected in the second part of Step 2. Again, different scenarios of lost sales, lost jobs and lost taxes will be presented depending on the assumed rates.

Step 9: Estimation of lost sales for IP right holders

In order to discover the value of lost sales for domestic IPR owners, the estimated value of products sold worldwide which are fake versions of these brands or patents are combined with information on (1) the share of primary and secondary markets for these products by destination economy; and (2) consumers' substitution rates (see Step 8).

The calculation is very close to the one described in Step 4, with the only exception being that it is first performed by destination economy before being aggregated. The total value of lost sales for domestic right owners is given by adding the value of sales of fake products on primary markets to the value of sales on the secondary market, adjusted for consumers' substitution rates.[11]

Step 10: Estimating lost jobs in the domestic manufacturing industry

This step requires estimating the extent to which employment in the UK manufacturing sector responds to changes in sales on export markets and on the domestic market. This is done by applying the econometric model developed in Step 5 (explained Annex A.3), to data specific to the manufacturing industries. The results of this estimation for the UK manufacturing sector are displayed in Table A.2 in the Annex. The estimated transmission rates between lost sales and jobs lost by the UK manufacturing industry are displayed in Table 1.3.

These transmission rates appear to vary considerably across UK manufacturing industries, ranging from 0.24% for raw hides, skin and leather (HS 41) to 0.64% for domestic manufactured machinery and mechanical appliances (HS 84). This confirms that a robust and industry-specific estimation of these transmission rates is crucial in order to assess properly the impact of global trade in counterfeit and pirated products on employment.

Table 1.3. Degree of employment response to sales variations, UK manufacturing sector, 2011-2013

HS category	Sales elasticity of employment*
Foodstuff (02-21)	0.64
Beverages (22)	0.43
Residues from the food industries (23)	0.51
Tobacco (24)	0.64
Salt; sulphur; earths and stone; lime and cement (25)	0.53
Ores, slag and ash (26)	0.64
Mineral fuels (27)	0.48
Organic and inorganic chemicals (28/29)	0.54
Pharmaceutical products (30)	0.61
Fertilisers (31)	0.39
Tanning or dyeing extracts (32)	0.54
Perfumery and cosmetics (33)	0.54
Soap; albuminoidal substances; glues; explosives (34-37)	0.56
Miscellaneous chemical products (38)	0.43
Plastic and articles thereof (39)	0.63
Rubber and article thereof (40)	0.56
Raw hides, skins and leather (41)	0.24
Articles of leather; handbags (42)	0.41
Furskins and artificial fur (43)	0.38
Wood and articles thereof (44)	0.59
Cork; straw and articles thereof (45/46)	0.45
Pulp and paper (47/48)	0.59

Table 1.3. Degree of employment response to sales variations, UK manufacturing sector, 2011-2013 (*continued*)

HS category	Sales elasticity of employment*
Printed articles (49)	0.64
Silk; wool; and other vegetable textile fibres (50-53)	0.48
Man-made filaments and staple fibres (54/55)	0.64
Wadding; cordage; ropes and articles thereof (56)	0.25
Carpets and rugs (57)	0.47
Finishing of textiles (58)	0.46
Other textiles n.e.c. (59)	0.48
Knitted or crocheted fabrics (60)	0.28
Clothing, knitted or crocheted (61)	0.46
Clothing and accessories, not knitted or crocheted (62/65)	0.57
Other made-up textile articles (63)	0.54
Footwear (64)	0.43
Articles of stone, plaster and cement (68)	0.58
Ceramic products (69)	0.55
Glass and glassware (70)	0.54
Jewellery (71)	0.47
Iron and steel; and articles thereof (72/73)	0.58
Copper; nickel; aluminium; lead; zinc; tin; and articles thereof (74-81)	0.61
Tools and cutlery of base metal (82)	0.57
Miscellaneous articles of base metal (83)	0.59
Machinery and mechanical appliances (84)	0.64
Electrical machinery and electronics (85)	0.63
Railway (86)	0.50
Vehicles (87)	0.61
Aircraft (88)	0.62
Ships (89)	0.59
Optical; photographic; medical apparatus (90)	0.64
Watches (91)	0.23
Musical instruments (92)	0.24
Arms and ammunition (93)	0.56
Furniture (94)	0.62
Toys and games (95)	0.51
Miscellaneous manufactured articles (66/67/96)	0.55

Note: *The sales elasticity of employment indicates the scale of drop in employment (in percentage), as a consequence of a one-percent drop in sales.

Step 11: Estimating taxes foregone

Unlike counterfeit and pirated imports, jobs lost due to infringements of IPRs affect only three types of tax revenues: corporate income taxes (CIT) of right holders; and social security contributions (SSC) and personal income taxes (PIT) paid by employers and employees in the manufacturing sector. The value-added taxes (VAT) on domestic sales of residents' IPR-infringing products are not calculated, since they have already taken into account when estimating the value of foregone tax revenues induced by lost sales due to counterfeit and pirated imports.

The methodologies applied to calculate each of these foregone tax revenues are exactly the same than those described in Step 6. Again, this is done industry by industry in order to obtain as accurate estimates as possible.

Notes

1. The Harmonized System (HS) is an international commodity classification system, developed and maintained by the World Customs Organization.

2. Each type of fake product and its associated trademark or patent.

3. Formally, let s_c and $\bar{s}_c$ denote, respectively, the import value and quantity of any custom seizure of counterfeit products, with $c \in \{1, \ldots, N\}$ the range of customs seizures, and N their total number. $p_c = s_c/\bar{s}_c$ then refers to the unit value of each custom seizure, and can serve as a proxy for their unit price. Let $p_{bp} = \left(\sum_{c\in\{bp\}} p_c\right)/N_{bp}$ defines the (unweighted) price average of any type of product p associated with the brand or patent b, with N_{bp} the total number of custom seizures reported for this "product category - brand" combination. The standard deviation of this price is denoted σ_{bp} .

   X_c is defined as a dichotomous (binary) variable that takes the value of 0 if the fake goods included in the seized shipment were intended to be sold on the primary market, or 1 if they were intended to be sold on the secondary market. In accordance with the arguments mentioned in the main text, X_c is assumed to be defined as follows:

$$X_c \begin{cases} = 0 \text{ if } p_c \in \left[p_{bp} - \dfrac{1.96 \times \sigma_{bp}}{\sqrt{N_{bp}}};\ \max\limits_{c\in\{bp\}} p_c \right] \\ = 1 \text{ if } p_c \epsilon \left[\min\limits_{c\epsilon\{bp\}} p_c;\ p_{bp} - \dfrac{1.96 \times \sigma_{bp}}{\sqrt{N_{bp}}} \right[\end{cases}$$

$\forall c\{bp\}$. It follows that the share of products sold on the primary market can be calculated by product category, τ_p^1, and/or for the entire mass of fake imports, and is given by:

$$\left(\sum_b \sum_c x_c s_c\right) / \left(\sum_b \sum_c s_c\right), \quad \forall c\epsilon\{bp\}$$

4. In two distinct studies, Rob and Waldfogel (2006, 2007) found, for instance, a displacement rate between illegal recorded music and video purchases and legitimate ones of around 20% and 67%, respectively, for a sample of US undergraduate students in 2005. Other academic studies of the recorded music industry suggest a displacement rate between 15% and 20% (Liebowitz, 2006; Zentner, 2006; Michel, 2006; Oberholzer-Gee and Strumpf, 2007). This means that every 5-6 illegal downloads displaces a legal sale.

5. The purposes of this exercise were: (i) to assess the proportion of consumers who, when given the opportunity to purchase either a counterfeit or legitimate version of consumer goods, would choose to purchase the counterfeit item; (ii) to determine their product attitudes; and (iii) to obtain demographic characteristics.

6. Note that 39% of the sample stated that they had knowingly purchased counterfeit products; 61% stated that they have never knowingly purchased counterfeit goods.

7. The remaining share of consumers is split as follows: 45% of fake buyers would not have bought anything and 16% would have bought another fake item in the case of clothing and footwear. These figures are 39% and 33%, respectively, in the case of watches; and 37% and

   14%, respectively, in the case of fragrance. No additional investigation about potential price differences between genuine and fake offerings was made.

8. More formally, the principle behind the measure of consumer detriment is as follows. First, for any type of product p related to the brand b, the average price paid on primary market, p_{bp}^1, and the average price paid on secondary market, p_{bp}^2, are calculated. Since the gap between these prices represents the "value of consumers' deception", it can be used as a proxy for consumer detriment of purchasing a given

branded product bp on the primary market: $d_{bp} = p^1_{bp} - p^2_{bp}$. Finally, these detriments can be aggregated by product category, or at the national level, multiplying them by the estimated volume of sales on primary markets, "Q^1_{bp}, as follows: $D = \sum_b \sum_p \left(d_{bp} Q^1_{bp}\right)$.

9. Formally, for each product type p, the loss of sales incurred by domestic wholesalers and retailers due to counterfeit and pirated imports, S_p, is given by adding the estimated value of counterfeit and pirated imports sold on the primary market – i.e. the total value of counterfeit and pirated imports, C_p, estimated in Step 1, times the share of the primary market, τ^1_p , estimated in Step 2 – to the estimated value of fakes sold on the secondary market times the consumers' substitution rates, ρ_p:

$$S_p = \left[\tau^1_p \times C_p\right] + \left[(1 - \tau^1_p) \times C_p \times \rho_p\right]$$

10. More formally, the estimated transmission rates between sales and jobs, ε_p, allow recovering the number of lost jobs as follows. First, the share of lost jobs due to counterfeit and pirated imports into the total employment within each retail and wholesale industry, ϑ_p, is calculated by multiplying the share of lost sales into the total sales of genuine products in the industry, $S_p/\hat{S}_p$, with the transmission rates:

$$\vartheta_p = \varepsilon_p \times \left(S_p/\hat{S}_p\right)$$

Second, these shares of lost jobs are applied onto data on the level of employment, $\hat{L}_p$. This give us the amount of lost jobs in the wholesale and retail industries due to counterfeit and pirated imports, J_p:

$$J_p = \vartheta_p \times \hat{L}_p$$

11. Formally, by denoting τ^1_{pd} the share of the primary market in destination economy d for all products of type p that infringe residents' IPR, and C_{pd} the estimated value of fake sales of those products in that destination, the estimated value of lost sales for domestic right holders by product category p is given by:

$$S_p = \sum_d \left[\tau^1_{pd} \times C_{pd}\right] + \left[(1 - \tau^1_{pd}) \times C_{pd} \times \rho_p\right]$$

with ρ_p denoting the product type-specific consumers' substitution rates.

References

Anti-Counterfeiting Group (2007), "Consumer survey – Watch sector; commissioned from independent survey specialists", Lebury Research.

Bian, X., Haque, S. and Smith, A. (2015), "Social power, product conspicuousness and the demand for luxury brand counterfeit products", *British Journal of Social Psychology*, 54(1): 37-54.

Bian, X., Wang, K-Y., Smith, A. and Yannopoulou, N. (2016), "New insights into unethical counterfeit consumption", *Journal of Business Research,* 69(10): 4249-4258.

Eisend, M. and Schuchert-Güler, P. (2006), "Explaining counterfeit purchases, a review and preview", *Academy of Marketing Science Review*, 12: 1–25.

Electrical Safety First (2016), "A shocking rip off: The true cost of counterfeit electrical products", Electrical Safety First, London, www.electricalsafetyfirst.org.uk/mediafile/100492991/True-Cost-of-a-Counterfeit.pdf.

OECD/EUIPO (2016), *Trade in Counterfeit and Pirated Goods: Mapping the Economic Impact*, OECD Publishing, Paris, http://dx.doi.org/10.1787/9789264252653-en.

Tom, G., Garibaldi, B., Zeng, Y., and J. Pilcher (1998), "Consumer demand for counterfeit goods", *Psychology & Marketing*, 15(5), 405-421.

WIPO (2016a), *Global Brand Database*, World Intellectual Property Office, Geneva, www.wipo.int/branddb/en/, accessed in 2016.

WIPO (2016b), *PATENTSCOPE Database: International and National Patent Collection*, World Intellectual Property Office, Geneva, https://patentscope.wipo.int/search/en/search.jsf, accessed in 2016.

Yoo, B. and Lee, S. H. (2009), "Buy genuine luxury fashion products or counterfeits?", *NA-Advances in Consumer Research,* Volume 36.

Chapter 2.

The effects of trade in fake goods on the UK economy

This chapter presents the quantitative assessment of effects of counterfeit trade on the UK economy, based on the methodology presented in Chapter 1. It quantifies: 1) the impacts on the UK of imported fake products; and 2) impacts of worldwide trade in goods that infringe the IP of UK rights holders. For both these impact pathways it quantifies the effect on consumers, sales, jobs and government revenues. It also outlines global trends in trade in counterfeits of products of relevance to the United Kingdom.

This chapter presents the quantitative assessment of effects of counterfeit trade on the UK economy, based on the methodology presented in Chapter 1. There are two contexts for the assessment:

1. Impacts on the UK of imported fake products
2. Impacts of worldwide trade in goods that infringe the IP of UK rights holders.

What are the direct impacts in the UK of imported fake products?

The first step consists of quantifying the volume of counterfeit and pirated goods imported by the UK economy. This assessment draws on a unified database on customs seizures of products whose customs forms indicate the UK as the destination.[1] The data were received from the European Commission's customs officers (DG TAXUD) for the period 2011-2013. Because the value of counterfeit and pirated products seized by customs authorities is likely to represent only a fraction of the actual value of fakes imported by the UK, this section uses the GTRIC methodology developed in OECD-EUIPO (2016) and described in detail in the first step of Chapter 1 to provide a reasonable estimate of the full value of imported fakes.

Where do fake products arriving in the UK mainly come from?

A review of the data on customs seizures shows that Asian economies were the main provenance of counterfeit and pirated products imported by the UK over the period 2011-2013 (Figure 2.1.). In particular, China, Hong-Kong (China) and India were the top three provenance economies of fake UK imports, representing respectively around 85%, 10% and 2% of all customs seizures of products referring to the UK as final destination.

Figure 2.1. Top provenance economies of counterfeit imports to the UK, 2011-2013

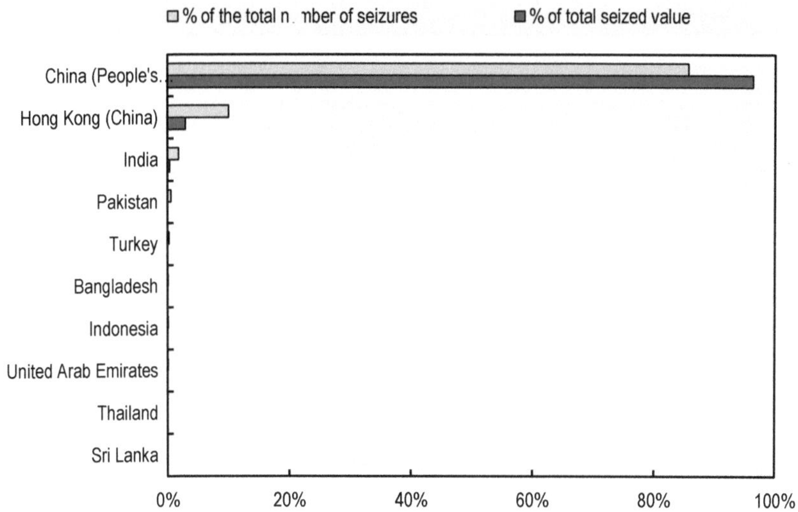

StatLink http://dx.doi.org/10.1787/888933553157

In order to compare the propensities of each provenance country to be a source of counterfeit and pirated goods sold in the UK, these data on customs seizures need to be compared with data on each of the country's UK imports of genuine products. This was done using the GTRIC-e index, which compares customs seizures intensities of counterfeit and pirated products shipped from a given provenance economy with the share of that provenance economy in UK imports. GTRIC-e assigns a high score to an economy which is a source of a high value of counterfeit products in absolute terms, or when a large share of UK imports from that economy is counterfeit.

Table 2.1 shows the top ten economies most likely to be a provenance of counterfeit and pirated products for the UK over the period 2011-2013 (see Table B.1 in Annex B for a complete list). Clearly, some of these provenance economies appear to be huge sources of infringing items, led notably by China and Hong Kong, China. Note that this could be because they are either important producers of counterfeit and pirated goods, or because they are strategic points of transit.

Table 2.1. The 15 economies most likely to export counterfeit and pirated products to the UK

GTRIC-e average; 2011-2013

Provenance economy	GTRIC-e
Hong Kong (China)	1.000
China (People's Republic of)	1.000
Pakistan	0.900
India	0.644
Syrian Arab Republic	0.590
Bangladesh	0.358
Malaysia	0.325
United Arab Emirates	0.307
Indonesia	0.265
Turkey	0.26
Singapore	0.236
Thailand	0.224
Italy	0.186
Egypt	0.173
Poland	0.167

Notes: A high GTRIC-e score indicates that an economy has a high propensity to be a source of counterfeits and pirated products imported into the UK, either in absolute terms, or as a share of UK imports. The results for all provenance economies over the period 2011-2013 are reported in Table B.1 in Annex B.

Which imported products are most likely to be counterfeit or pirated?

The unified dataset on customs seizures of counterfeit and pirated goods can also be used to quantify infringed product categories within UK imports. It should be noted that over the period 2011-2013, a large range of product categories imported into the UK was subject to counterfeiting (see Figure 2.2). This means that any type of product for which IP adds economic value to rights holders, and thus creates price differentials, becomes a target for counterfeiters and a potential threat to the UK economy and society.

While a broad range of goods among UK imports are sensitive to infringement, the intensity of counterfeiting varies significantly across product categories. This is supported by seizures statistics shown in Figure 2.2, which are concentrated in a relatively limited number of product categories, including footwear (HS 64), electrical machinery and equipment (HS 85), and articles of leather and handbags (HS 42).

Figure 2.2. The main product categories likely to be counterfeit within UK imports, 2011-2013

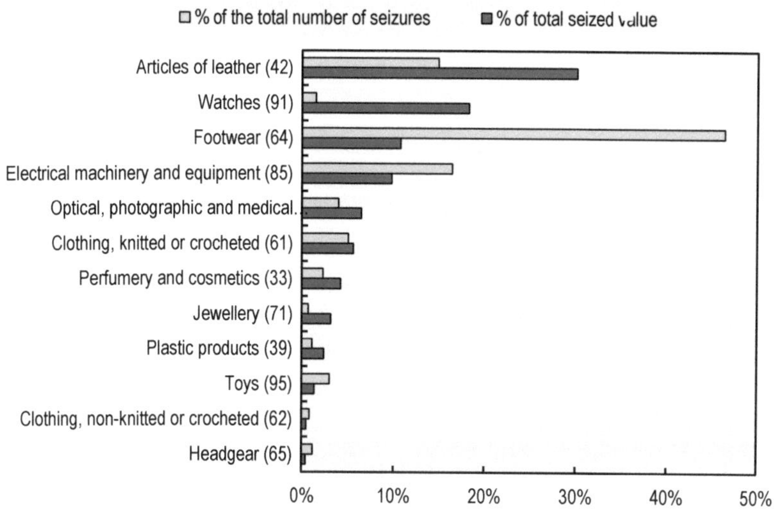

StatLink http://dx.doi.org/10.1787/888933553176

In order to obtain a meaningful measure of the propensity for different types of infringing products to be shipped to the UK, the GTRIC-p index was used. This index compares the likelihood of goods in each product category to be counterfeit. Similar to GTRIC-e, this is done by comparing global customs seizures intensities of a given product category with the share of this product category in UK imports. The result is a ranking of products imported to the UK according to the likelihood that they will be counterfeit (See Table B.2. in Annex B).

Table 2.2. The 15 UK import product categories most likely to be counterfeit

HS category	GTRIC-p
Articles of leather; handbags (42)	1.000
Footwear (64)	1.000
Watches (91)	1.000
Perfumery and cosmetics (33)	0.999
Clothing, knitted or crocheted (61)	0.994
Optical; photographic; medical apparatus (90)	0.977
Miscellaneous manufactured articles (66/67/96)	0.946
Toys and games (95)	0.760
Electrical machinery and electronics (85)	0.708
Plastic and articles thereof (39)	0.681
Tools and cutlery of base metal (82)	0.657
Pharmaceutical products (30	0.474
Clothing and accessories, not knitted or crocheted (62/65)	0.367
Other made-up textile articles (63)	0.336
Jewellery (71)	0.329

Notes: A high GTRIC-p score implies a product category that is more likely to be counterfeit, i.e. it contains high values of counterfeit imports in GBP, or a large share of UK imports of that product category is counterfeit. The results for all product categories over the period 2011-2013 are reported in Table B.2. in Annex B.

What is the total value of counterfeit imports to the UK?

The best estimates – based on the data provided by customs authorities and on the GTRIC methodology – indicate that **counterfeit and pirated imports to the UK accounted for as much as GBP 9.3 billion in 2013, the equivalent of 4% of UK imports.** The term "as much as" is crucial in this context as it refers to the upper boundary of counterfeit and pirated UK imports. World trade and its structure are very dynamic, especially in the aftermath of the 2008-2009 global financial crisis, so this percentage cannot be directly applied to values for other years. In addition, this amount concerns only tangible goods and does not include domestically produced and consumed counterfeit products.

The analysis also reveals that the intensity of counterfeiting and piracy within UK imports varies considerably across product categories. In absolute terms, electronic and electrical equipment (HS 85) was by far the most counterfeit imported type of goods, with an estimated value of GBP 2.4 billion of fakes imported to the UK in

2013. In relative terms, articles of leather and handbags (HS 42), toys and games (HS 95) and clothing (HS 61) were most targeted by counterfeiters, with fakes accounting for 16.7%, 14.7% and 14.5% respectively of imports from these product categories (Figure 2.3).

Figure 2.3. Estimates of counterfeit and pirated imports to the UK

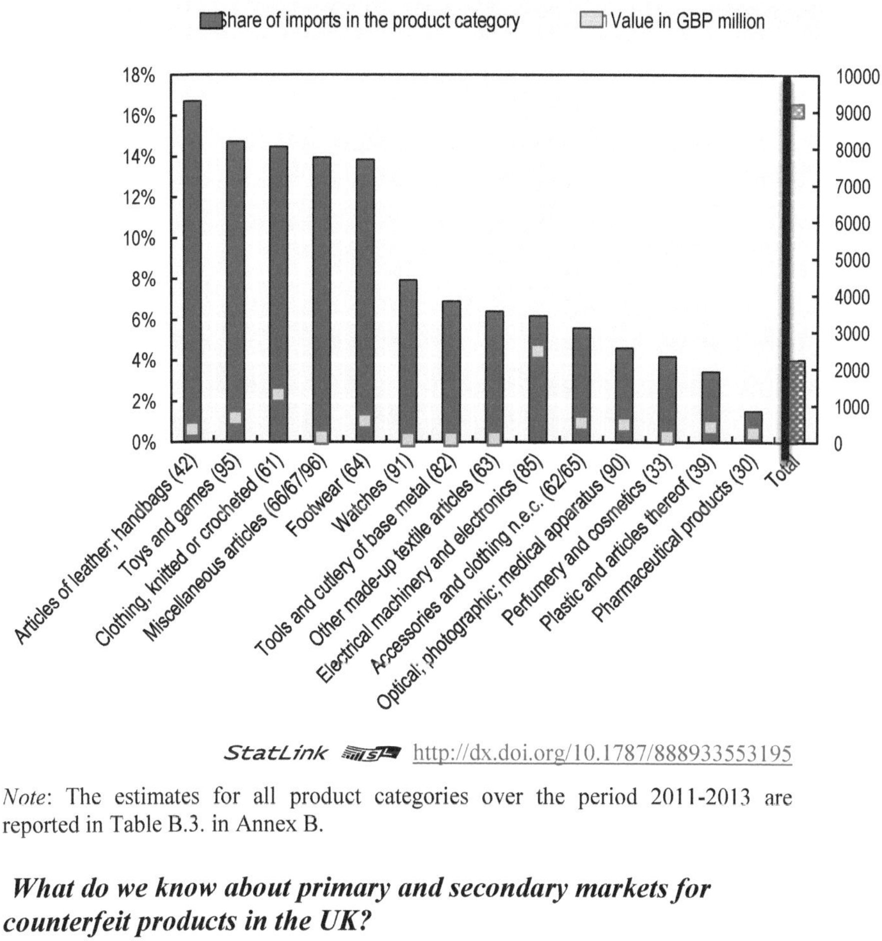

StatLink http://dx.doi.org/10.1787/888933553195

Note: The estimates for all product categories over the period 2011-2013 are reported in Table B.3. in Annex B.

What do we know about primary and secondary markets for counterfeit products in the UK?

Table 2.3 identifies the primary and secondary markets within the UK for each product category. This shows that nearly half (47.7%) of counterfeit and pirated imports to the UK over the period 2011-2013 were destined for sale in the secondary market (for consumers looking for fake products). The other half were therefore unwittingly bought by consumers. The share of fakes destined for secondary markets varies significantly by product, ranging from 11.1% for foodstuff (HS 02-21) to 61% for optical, photographic and medical instruments (HS 90).

Table 2.1. Share of counterfeit and pirated imports sold on secondary markets within the UK, 2011-2013

HS category	Share of customs seizures destined for secondary market
Foodstuff (02-21)	11.11%
Pharmaceutical products (30)	29.81%
Tanning or dyeing extracts; putty and inks (32)	48.00%
Perfumery and cosmetics (33)	55.95%
Plastic and plastic products (39)	32.57%
Articles of leather; handbags (42)	35.54%
Wood and paper products (47/48)	49.10%
Printed articles (49)	33.33%
Special woven fabrics; tapestries; embroidery (58)	25.00%
Knitted or crocheted fabrics (60)	43.14%
Clothing, knitted or crocheted (61)	55.47%
Clothing and accessories, non-knitted or crocheted (62/65)	23.65%
Other made-up textile articles (63)	51.61%
Footwear (64)	48.29%
Ceramic products (69)	52.00%
Glass and glassware (60)	16.67%
Jewellery (71)	42.86%
Tools and cutlery of base metal (82)	40.28%
Miscellaneous articles of base metal (83)	45.95%
Machinery and mechanical appliances (84)	58.00%
Electronic and electrical equipment (85)	58.21%
Vehicles and parts (87)	20.59%
Optical, photographic and medical instruments (90)	61.03%
Watches (91)	34.24%
Furniture (94)	33.33%
Toys (95)	41.18%
Miscellaneous manufactured articles (96/66/67)	27.64%
Total	**47.71%**

Given that to the extent of our knowledge no academic research has so far tried to empirically estimate these figures, the plausibility of these results can only be tested by comparing them with the few consumer surveys available. These corroborate these findings. The Gallup Organisation, for instance, conducted consumer surveys on behaviours towards counterfeiting in 2007 on 2 800 residents in 14 EU countries aged 18 and over and 1 304 US adults. It found that of those who had bought a counterfeit good, only 52.6% were aware that the product was a fake before they bought it (The Gallup Organisation, 2007). This result is very close to the estimated 47.7% share of the secondary market in this study.

The Gallup consumer survey also confirms that the share of the secondary market varies substantially across product categories (Table 2.4.). For instance, the share of consumers having knowingly bought counterfeit products is 51% for brand name fashion clothing (compared to 55.4% in this study), while it is significantly lower for brand name watches, at 39.2% of consumers (42.7% in this study).

Table 2.4. Share of consumers in the EU and the US having knowingly bought counterfeit products, 2007

Product type	Share of the secondary market
Brand name fashion clothing	50.80%
Brand name watches	39.20%
Music CDs or audio cassettes	51.10%
Movies (VHS, VCDs, DVDs)	45.10%
Computer operating systems	58.90%
Computer application software	49.40%
Video games	38.40%
Pharmaceuticals or medicines	46.80%
Alcoholic beverages	28.50%
Tobacco	61.60%
Tools and auto parts	39.50%
Jewellery	53.40%
Total	**52.60%**

Note: The exact question was: "Prior to purchasing, were you aware it was an imitation or counterfeit product?"
Source: The Gallup Organisation (2007), Global Consumer Awareness, Attitudes, and Opinions on Counterfeiting and Piracy.

To what extent are consumers overpaying for fake products?

While consumers who knowingly purchase fake products are prepared to accept any trade-off between cost and quality, consumers who unwittingly purchase fake goods end up paying an excess price for a low quality product. As explained in Step 3 in Chapter 1, this "consumer detriment" can be estimated by the price premium earned by counterfeiters from both markets, times the volume of fake goods sold on primary markets.

The estimates for consumer detriments in the UK were calculated in two steps: first, for each sector the difference between average prices on primary and secondary markets was calculated. These differences represent the individual consumer detriment from an individual purchase. Second, this individual detriment was multiplied by the total volume of transactions on primary market in a given industry.

The estimates for consumer detriments in the UK are presented in Table 2.5. In 2013, the highest detriments were recorded for "clothing, footwear, leather and related products" (GBP 54.1 million) and watches and jewellery (GBP 25.8 million). The total detriment due to consumer deception in 2013 amounted to almost GBP 100 million.

Table 2.5. Estimates of consumers' detriment by sector, 2011-2013

In GBP million

Year	2011	2012	2013
Class			
Food, beverages and tobacco	0.00	0.06	0.06
Chemical and allied products; except pharmaceuticals, perfumery and cosmetics	0.09	0.01	0.03
Pharmaceutical and medicinal chemical products	1.10	0.59	0.59
Perfumery and cosmetics	1.99	2.84	1.69
Textiles and other intermediate products (e.g. plastics; rubbers; paper; wood)	3.56	3.96	3.65
Clothing, footwear, leather and related products	52.1	47.9	54.1
Watches and jewellery	16.1	16.9	25.8
Non-metallic mineral products (e.g. glass and glass products, ceramic products)	0.00	0.00	0.01
Basic metals and fabricated metal products (except machinery and equipment)	0.14	0.46	0.3
Electrical household appliances, electronic and telecommunications equipment	5.34	8.05	10.2

Table 2.5. Estimates of consumers' detriment by sector, 2011-2013 *(continued)*

In GBP million

Year	2011	2012	2013
Class			
Machinery. computers and peripheral equipment; ships and aircrafts	2.23	0.05	2.83
Motor vehicles and motorcycles	0.22	0.09	0.21
Household cultural and recreation goods	0.29	0.34	0.37
Furniture, lighting equipment, carpets and other manufacturing n.e.c	0.07	0.14	0.11
Total	**83.23**	**81.4**	**99.96**

How are fake goods affecting sales in the UK retail and wholesale sector?

The sales lost to counterfeit and pirated imports for the retail and wholesale sector are calculated using the methodology presented in Step 4 in Chapter 1. Table 2.6. summarises the results for three scenarios for consumers' substitution rates between the fake goods and their genuine equivalent (c.f. Table 1.1. in Chapter 1). The estimated losses for the three scenarios are very close, which confirms the robustness of all the results presented below.

The highest sale losses to the UK wholesale and retail industries in absolute terms were for "clothing, footwear, leather and related products" (GBP 1.53 billion foregone sales in 2013 for Scenario 1), followed by "electrical household appliances, electronics and telecommunications" (GBP 1.20 billion in foregone sales in 2013 for Scenario 1). These two sectors also experienced the highest losses in relative terms – more than 10% and 5% respectively of foregone sales due to counterfeit and pirated imports.

Overall, the total volume of foregone sales in the UK wholesale and retail sector due to counterfeit and pirated imports in 2013 was GBP 4.218 billion for Scenario 1. This is equivalent to 1.37% of total sales in the UK wholesale and retail sector in that year.

Table 2.6. Lost sales for the UK retail and wholesale sector due to counterfeit and pirated imports, 2013

	Scenario 1		Scenario 2		Scenario 3	
Sector \ Unit	Value in GBP mn	Share of sales	Value in GBP mn	Share of sales	Value in GBP mn	Share of sales
Food, beverages and tobacco	21.3	0.05%	19.3	0.04%	16.1	0.02%
Chemical and allied products	4.3	0.14%	4.0	0.13%	3.8	0.12%
Pharmaceuticals	77.1	0.73%	66.6	0.63%	56.2	0.53%
Perfumery and cosmetics	72.8	1.52%	65.7	1.38%	59.7	1.25%
Textiles and other intermediate products	252.0	2.06%	250.0	2.05%	247	2.03%
Clothing, footwear, leather and related products	1530.0	5.06%	1400.0	4.63%	1350	4.49%
Watches and jewellery	141.0	4.20%	132.1	3.95%	134	4.01%
Non-metallic mineral products	10.2	0.20%	9.2	0.18%	8.1	0.16%
Basic metals and fabricated metal products	62.9	0.81%	60.4	0.78%	58.0	0.75%
Electrical appliances, electronics and telecom.	1240.1	10.10%	1160.0	9.38%	1070.0	8.66%
Machinery; computers and peripheral equipment; ships and aircrafts	187.0	0.67%	185.0	0.66%	183.0	0.65%
Motor vehicles and motorcycles	74.8	0.17%	73.8	0.17%	72.7	0.17%
Household cultural and recreation goods	374.0	3.60%	356.0	3.44%	339.1	3.27%
Furniture, lighting equipment, and other n.e.c	171.1	0.49%	167.1	0.48%	164.0	0.47%
Total	4218.4	1.37%	3951	1.28%	3766.8	1.22%

Note: In scenario 1, a substitution rate of 39 % has been chosen for product category related to clothing and footwear, 49% for products related to the perfumery and cosmetics sector, 27% for products belonging to the watch and jewellery industries, and 32% for all other fake products sold on secondary markets. Scenario 2 assumes substitution rates 10 percentage points lower, and scenario 3 assumes the substitution rates to be 20 percentage points lower than in the scenario 1.

How are fake goods affecting jobs in the UK retail and wholesale industry?

Lower sales in the retail and wholesale industries reduce demand for labour, and consequently lead to job losses. The basic econometric model presented in Chapter 1 (Step 5) allows us to estimate these losses. This is done by combining the estimated lost sales presented above with the industry-specific elasticities of employment linked to sales displayed in Table 1.2.

Table 2.7. below presents the main results for various branches of the wholesale and retail sector. In absolute terms, the highest job losses (19 700 in 2013) were found for the sales of textiles and other intermediate products. In relative terms, the highest job losses were in the clothing, footwear, leather and related products retail and wholesale sector, with 5.3% of employees affected by counterfeiting and piracy.

The total job losses in the retail and wholesale sector due to counterfeiting and piracy in 2013 amounted to more than 40 000, equivalent to more than 3% of all people employed in the sector.

Table 2.7. Lost jobs in the UK retail and wholesale sectors due to counterfeit and pirated imports, 2013

	Scenario 1		Scenario 2		Scenario 3	
Sector \ Unit	Number of employees	Share of employees	Number of employees	Share of employees	Number of employees	Share of employees
Food, beverages and tobacco	2045	1.13%	1991	1.03%	1977	0.97%
Chemical and allied products	1012	2.87%	955	2.54%	899	2.21%
Pharmaceuticals	432	0.65%	373	0.56%	315	0.47%
Perfumery and cosmetics	4778	2.38%	4314	2.67%	3920	2.06%
Textiles and other intermediate products	19709	3.37%	19543	3.28%	19379	3.18%
Clothing, footwear, and leather	7842	5.30%	7184	5.19%	6955	5.15%
Watches and jewellery	493	1.01%	464	0.95%	471	0.91%
Non-metallic mineral products	240	0.27%	215	0.24%	192	0.21%
Basic metals and fabricated metal products	936	0.95%	899	0.91%	863	0.87%
Electrical household appliances, electronics and telecommunications	640	2.24%	615	2.22%	691	2.21%
Machinery; computers and peripheral equipment; ships and aircrafts	10	0.00%	9	0.00%	9	0.00%
Motor vehicles and motorcycles	98	0.02%	96	0.02%	95	0.02%
Household cultural and recreation goods;	112	0.55%	106	0.51%	102	0.49%
Furniture, lighting equipment, and n.e.c.	2048	0.32%	2006	0.31%	1965	0.30%
Total	**40395**	**1.08%**	**37741**	**0.95%**	**36238**	**0.89%**

Note: In scenario 1, a substitution rate of 39 % has been chosen for product category related to clothing and footwear, 49% for products related to the perfumery and cosmetics sector, 27% for products belonging to the watch and jewellery industries, and 32% for all other fake products sold on secondary markets. Scenario 2 assumes substitution rates 10 percentage points lower, and scenario 3 assumes the substitution rates to be 20 percentage points lower than in the scenario 1.

What does the sale of fake goods mean for losses in government revenues?

Lower sales in the wholesale and retail sector due to counterfeit and pirated imports mean lower tax revenues for the government from value-added tax (VAT) revenue, corporate income tax (CIT), personal income tax revenues and social security contributions (see Step 6 in Chapter 1).

Table 2.8. presents these foregone tax revenues by types of taxes, which amounted to GBP 2.41 billion in 2013. Within this overall figure, the largest component was the foregone corporate income tax, amounting to GBP 1.44 billion.

Table 2.8. Public revenue losses due to counterfeit and pirated imports, 2013

	Scenario 1	Scenario 2	Scenario 3
Personal income taxes	48.8	45.8	43.8
Social security contributions	67.3	62.9	60.2
Corporate taxes	1451.4	1353.1	1292.7
Value-added taxes	843.4	789.4	753.3
Total	**2411**	**2251.1**	**2150.1**
Share of governmental taxes	**0.57%**	**0.54%**	**0.51%**

Note: In scenario 1, a substitution rate of 39 % has been chosen for product category related to clothing and footwear, 49% for products related to the perfumery and cosmetics sector, 27% for products belonging to the watch and jewellery industries, and 32% for all other fake products sold on secondary markets. Scenario 2 assumes substitution rates 10 percentage points lower, and scenario 3 assumes the substitution rates to be 20 percentage points lower than in the scenario 1.

What are the impacts of worldwide trade in fakes on UK IPR holders?

The first step in answering this question is to estimate the value of counterfeit and pirated goods traded worldwide that infringe IP rights of UK right holders. This assessment was done using a unified database of customs seizures associated with trademarks and patents whose holders' location address was registered in the UK during the period 2011-2013. In order to gauge the value of global counterfeiting and piracy infringing UK-related IP rights from this database, we relied on the GTRIC methodology developed in OECD/EUIPO (2016) adapted for exports and domestic sales, as explained in Step 7 of Chapter 1.

Interestingly, a review of the data on customs seizures highlights that the UK itself was the top destination for counterfeit and pirated products that infringe the IP rights of UK residents (Figure 2.4., Graph B), in terms of the number of customs seizures and the second destination in terms of seized value. This is followed by other northern European economies, including the Netherlands, Germany, Belgium; and Eastern European economies, such as the Czech Republic and Hungary (Figure 2.4., Graph B). Asian economies, particularly China, India and Turkey, were the main provenance of counterfeit and pirated goods that infringed IPs of UK residents over the period 2011-2013 (see Figure 2.4., Graph A).

In order to obtain a meaningful measure of the propensity for each economy to be a destination for counterfeit and pirated products whose IP rights are held by UK residents, these data on customs seizures need to be compared with data on UK exports of genuine products, and with data on UK domestic sales (for cases when these fake goods are going to be sold in the UK.) The GTRIC-e index was used, which compares customs seizures intensities of counterfeit and pirated products shipped to a given economy with the share of this economy in UK domestic production (exports plus domestic sales).

Figure 2.4. Top provenance and destination economies for fake UK-IP registered products, 2013

A. Provenance economies

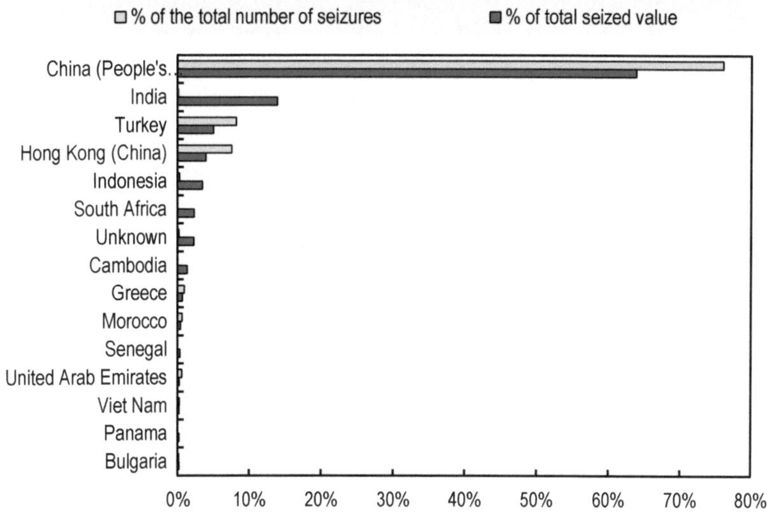

B. Destination economies

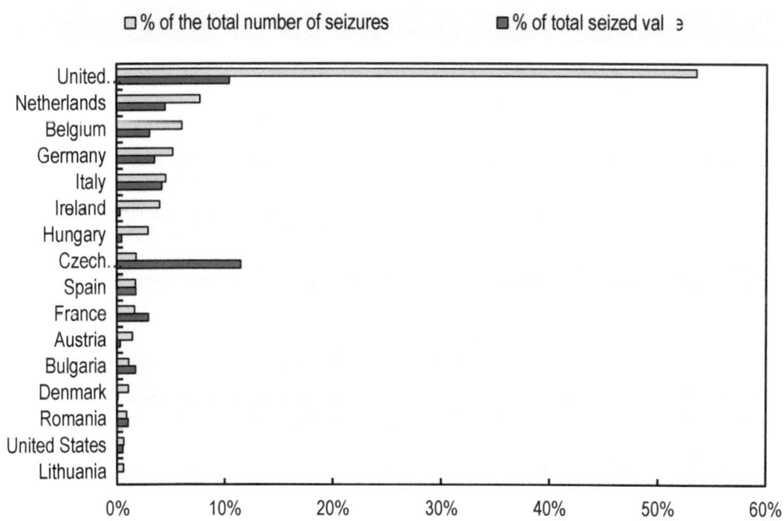

StatLink http://dx.doi.org/10.1787/888933553214

Table 2.9. lists the top 15 economies most likely to be a destination for counterfeit and pirated products infringing IP rights of UK holders over the period 2011-2013 (see Table B.5. in Annex B for a complete list). Interestingly, the most sensitive destination economies for this type of products are small Eastern and Southern European economies, including the Czech Republic, Malta, Bulgaria, Slovenia, San Marino, Portugal, Romania, Latvia and Estonia, as well as developing African economies such as the Democratic Republic of the Congo, Burkina Faso, Morocco and Togo.

Table 2.9. Top 15 economies most likely to import products infringing UK residents' rights

GTRIC-e, average 2011-2013

Destination economy	GTRIC-e
Czech Republic	0.970
Malta	0.966
Bulgaria	0.957
Slovenia	0.894
Democratic Republic of the Congo	0.882
San Marino	0.856
Portugal	0.822
Burkina Faso	0.820
Romania	0.815
Jordan	0.797
Comoros	0.791
Morocco	0.777
Latvia	0.738
Togo	0.723
Estonia	0.716
Italy	0.714

Note: A high GTRIC-e score indicates that an economy has a high propensity to import UK-IP registered products, either in absolute terms, or as a share of their imports. The results for all destination economies over the period 2011-2013 are reported in Table B.5. in Annex B.

Which types of UK-patented products are most susceptible to counterfeiting?

The unified dataset on customs seizures of counterfeit and pirated goods can also be used to understand for which product categories trademarks and patents of UK residents are the most vulnerable to global counterfeiting and piracy. Over the period 2011-2013, UK residents' IP rights were subject to counterfeiting and piracy for a large range of product categories, from basic common goods to luxury or intermediary products (see Figure 2.5.).

Although the scope of goods that are sensitive to IP infringement is broad, the intensity of counterfeiting and piracy targeting Trademarks and patents of UK residents varies significantly across product categories. Seizures statistics reported in Figure 2.5. indicate that UK-related IP rights infringements worldwide are especially concentrated in a limited number of industries. In terms of the number of customs seizures, these include electronics and electrical equipment (HS 85), clothing (HS 61 and 62) and articles of leather and handbags (HS 42). In terms of seized value, they also include footwear (HS 64), perfumery and cosmetics (HS 33) and headgear (HS 65).

Figure 2.5. Top product categories for fake UK products, 2011-2013

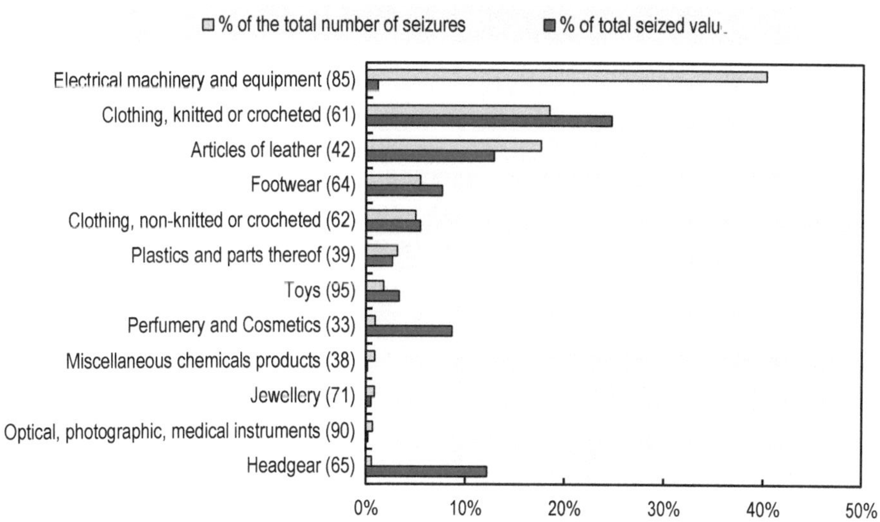

StatLink http://dx.doi.org/10.1787/888933553233

The GTRIC-p index was then used to compare which product categories are most to be vulnerable to counterfeiting and piracy. This compares for each product category, global customs seizures intensities of fakes infringing UK-related IP rights with the share of this product category in UK production (exports plus domestic sales). The result is a general ranking of industries according to their propensity to contain UK trademarks or patents that are sensitive to counterfeiting and piracy (Table 2.10.; see Table B.5. in Annex B for a complete list). A high GTRIC-p score implies either that a given product category contains high values of UK trademarks or patents that are sensitive to global counterfeiting and piracy in absolute terms (e.g. in GBP), or that a large share of the production of goods associated with a UK trademark or patent registered in this product category is counterfeit.

Table 2.10. The 15 product categories most sensitive to global counterfeiting in violation of UK trademarks or patents

GTRIC-p, average 2011-2013

HS category	GTRIC-p
Articles of leather; handbags (42)	1.000
Clothing, knitted or crocheted (61)	1.000
Clothing and accessories, not knitted or crocheted (62/65)	1.000
Footwear (64)	1.000
Tobacco (24)	1.000
Toys and games (95)	0.999
Knitted or crocheted fabrics (60)	0.951
Perfumery and cosmetics (33)	0.919
Watches (91)	0.870
Miscellaneous manufactured articles (66/67/96)	0.722
Pharmaceutical products (30)	0.719
Plastic and articles thereof (39)	0.542
Foodstuff (02-21)	0.359
Electrical machinery and electronics (85)	0.312
Other made-up textile articles (63)	0.302

Note: A high GTRIC-p score implies a product category that is more likely to be counterfeit, i.e. it contains high values of UK-IP registered products in monetary terms, or a large share of world imports of UK-IP registered goods of that product category is counterfeit. The results for all product categories over the period 2011-2013 are reported in Table B.5. in Annex B.

What is the value of global trade in counterfeit products that infringe UK IPRs?

The best estimates based on the data provided by customs authorities worldwide, and on the GTRIC methodology, indicate that **global trade in counterfeit products infringing UK trademarks and patents amounted to as much as GBP 13.4 billion in 2013, equivalent to 3% of total UK manufacturing sales (domestic plus exports).** Table 2.11. below breaks this amount down by product category and type of markets.

In absolute terms (i.e in GBP million), Trademarks and patents of UK residents related to pharmaceutical products (HS 30), vehicles and parts (HS 87) and jewellery (HS 71) were particularly targeted by counterfeiters and pirates in global trade. In relative terms, footwear (HS 64), clothing (HS 61) and tobacco (24) were the most often faked type of products worldwide, with fakes making up more than 10% of counterfeit goods within each category.

The last four columns of Table 2.11. break down the sales of UK IPR-infringing fake products into those made in the UK territory itself and those made in other provenance economies worldwide. Interestingly, GBP 5.8 billion of the estimated total GBP 13.4 billion were due to imports into the UK itself. The remaining share, GBP 7.6 billion, was due to world shipments of UK IPR-infringing fakes that were imported by third economies worldwide. This means that the majority of traded goods that infringe Trademarks and patents of UK residents are neither exported from nor imported by the UK.

Table 2.11. Estimates of trade in counterfeit products infringing UK residents' IP rights, 2013

Product type	All products		Products sold on the UK territory		Products sold outside the UK territory	
HS category\Unit	Value in GPB million	Share of total sales	Value in GPB million	Share of domestic sales	Value in GPB million	Share of exports
Foodstuff (02-21)	1030	4.14%	813	4.17%	217	4.04%
Beverages (22)	263	1.43%	174	1.54%	89	1.25%
Tobacco (24)	28	10.16%	0	0.00%	28	10.16%
Mineral fuels (27)	339	0.82%	0	4.17%	217	4.04%
Pharmaceutical products (30)	2280	7.47%	712	7.67%	1568	7.38%
Perfumery and cosmetics (33)	719	9.03%	361	9.26%	358	8.81%
Soap; glues; explosives (34-37)	36	0.78%	31	0.79%	5	0.70%
Miscellaneous chemical products (38)	178	3.17%	24	3.44%	154	3.13%
Plastic and articles thereof (39)	1160	6.01%	680	6.02%	480	6.00%
Rubber and article thereof (40)	136	2.83%	68	2.83%	68	2.83%
Articles of leather; handbags (42)	84	9.84%	18	9.73%	66	9.87%
Pulp and paper (47/48)	45	2.53%	0	0.00%	45	2.53%
Printed articles (49)	221	2.43%	159	2.51%	62	2.23%
Finishing of textiles (58)	17	3.03%	13	2.98%	4	3.20%
Knitted or crocheted fabrics (60)	22	9.67%	11	9.48%	11	9.86%
Clothing, knitted or crocheted (61)	220	10.07%	0	0.00%	220	10.07%
Clothing and accessories, not knitted or crocheted (62/65)	84	8.54%	0	0.00%	84	8.54%
Other made-up textile articles (63)	59	3.35%	36	3.55%	23	3.08%
Footwear (64)	157	10.42%	24	9.73%	133	10.55%

Table 2.11. Estimates of trade in counterfeit products infringing UK residents' IP rights, 2013 (*continued*)

Product type	All products		Products sold on the UK territory		Products sold outside the UK territory	
HS category\Unit	Value in GPB million	Share of total sales	Value in GPB million	Share of domestic sales	Value in GPB million	Share of exports
Ceramic products (69)	8	0.74%	5	0.76%	3	0.69%
Glass and glassware (70)	46	1.59%	34	1.60%	12	1.57%
Jewellery (71)	1250	1.77%	120	2.89%	1130	1.70%
Iron and steel (72/73)	97	0.74%	62	0.83%	35	0.61%
Tools and cutlery of base metal (82)	62	3.20%	36	3.36%	26	3.00%
Miscellaneous metal articles (83)	80	1.76%	65	1.78%	15	1.66%
Machinery; mechanical appliances (84)	998	1.30%	458	1.53%	540	1.16%
Electrical machinery; electronics (85)	1110	3.43%	439	3.66%	671	3.29%
Vehicles and parts (87)	1670	2.37%	934	2.55%	736	2.18%
Optical; photo.; medical apparatus (90)	536	2.57%	244	2.82%	292	2.38%
Watches (91)	34	6.11%	3	8.91%	31	5.96%
Musical instruments (92)	0.7	0.81%	0.2	0.85%	0.5	0.80%
Furnitures (94)	62	0.80%	47	0.83%	15	0.72%
Toys and games (95)	182	9.95%	54	9.73%	128	10.04%
Miscellaneous (66/67/96)	145	7.74%	138	7.70%	7	8.56%
Total	**13359**	**3.02%**	**5765**	**3.12%**	**7594**	**3.05%**

What do we know about primary and secondary markets for counterfeit UK products?

The next step consists of comparing the share of UK IPR-infringing fakes that are sold on primary markets worldwide with those that are sold on secondary markets. This is done using the methodology described in Step 2 (Chapter 1).

Table 2.12. identifies these markets by product category. The results indicate that between 2011 and 2013, 47.7% of UK IPR-infringing fakes that were traded worldwide were offered on primary markets, i.e. they were sold to unsuspecting consumers. This share varies between product categories, ranging from 30% for soap, albuminoidal substances, glues, and explosives (HS 34 to 37) to 87% for foodstuff (HS 02 to 21).

Table 2.12. Share of secondary markets for counterfeit products infringing UK patents and trademarks, 2011-2013

HS code	Share of customs seizures
Foodstuff (02-21)	13.10%
Beverages (22)	31.20%
Tobacco (24)	50.30%
Pharmaceutical products (30)	28.21%
Perfumery and cosmetics (33)	45.16%
Soap; albuminoidal substances; explosives (34-37)	69.93%
Miscellaneous chemical products (38)	56.08%
Articles of leather; handbags (42)	56.26%
Pulp and paper (47-48)	16.67%
Printed articles (49)	41.67%
Finishing of textiles (58)	47.30%
Knitted or crocheted fabrics (60)	41.18%
Clothing, knitted or crocheted (61)	57.78%
Clothing and accessories, non-knitted or crocheted (62/65)	61.74%
Other made-up textile articles (63)	71.43%
Footwear (64)	52.73%
Ceramic products (69)	65.90%
Glass and glassware (70)	22.76%
Jewellery (71)	47.18%
Iron and steel, and articles thereof (72/73)	62.80%
Tools and cutlery of base metal (82)	32.46%
Miscellaneous articles of base metal (83)	44.70%
Machinery and mechanical appliances (84)	47.50%
Electronic and electrical equipment (85)	66.91%
Vehicles and parts (87)	41.38%
Optical; photographic; medical apparatus (90)	61.85%
Watches (91)	53.33%
Musical instruments (92)	51.31%
Furniture (94)	37.75%
Toys (95)	44.57%
Miscellaneous manufactured articles (96/66/67)	54.06%
Total	**53.27%**

What does counterfeiting mean for lost sales by UK IPR owners?

What value of sales were never realised by UK right owners due to counterfeiting of their products? This was calculated following the methodology described in Step 7 (Chapter 1). As for the case of the retail and wholesale sector, three scenarios were estimated based on different assumed consumers' substitution rates (Table 2.13.).

The total volume of foregone sales by UK companies due to infringement of their IP rights in 2013 amounted to GBP 8.6 billion, or 1.95% of their total sales in that year. The manufacturing industries for pharmaceutical products and motor vehicles and motorcycles incurred the highest losses (respectively, GBP 1.51 and 1.25 billion of foregone sales in 2013). In terms of shares of sales, the highest losses were recorded by the perfumery and cosmetics industry, who would have lost 6.92% of their sales.

Table 2.13. Lost sales for UK right owners due to global trade in fake products infringing their IP rights, 2013

	Scenario 1		Scenario 2		Scenario 3	
Sector \ Unit	Value in GBP million	Share of sales	Value in GBP million	Share of sales	Value in GBP million	Share of sales
Food, beverages and tobacco	1058	2.54%	932	2.26%	917	2.08%
Chemical and allied products	90	0.97%	11.4	0.12%	7.8	0.08%
Pharmaceutical and medicinal chemical products	1508	5.26%	1500	5.25%	1450	5.07%
Perfumery and cosmetics	517	6.90%	517	6.92%	451	6.03%
Textiles and other intermediate products	915	3.62%	847	3.34%	842	3.32%
Clothing, footwear, leather	364	5.31%	364	5.31%	322	4.69%
Watches and jewellery	771	1.28%	772	1.28%	708	1.18%
Non-metallic mineral products	53	1.38%	523	1.38%	49	1.28%
Basic metals and fabricated metal products	111	0.61%	100	0.55%	98	0.54%
Electrical household appliances, electronics and telecommunications	834	1.73%	835	1.73%	774	1.61%

Table 2.13. Lost sales for UK right owners due to global trade in fake products infringing their IP rights, 2013 *(continued)*

	Scenario 1		Scenario 2		Scenario 3	
Sector \ Unit	Value in GBP million	Share of sales	Value in GBP million	Share of sales	Value in GBP million	Share of sales
Machinery, computers and peripheral equipment; ships and aircrafts	594	0.90%	593	0.90%	574	0.87%
Motor vehicles and motorcycles	1237	1.86%	1240	1.86%	1220	1.83%
Household cultural and recreation goods	281	2.70%	280	2.69%	268	2.57%
Furniture, lighting equipment, carpets and other manufacturing n.e.c	158	1.72%	158	1.72%	155	1.68%
Total	**8599.6**	**1.95%**	**8209.9**	**1.86%**	**7858.8**	**1.78%**

Note: In scenario 1, a substitution rate of 39 % has been chosen for product category related to clothing and footwear, 49% for products related to the perfumery and cosmetics sector, 27% for products belonging to the watch and jewellery industries, and 32% for all other fake products sold on secondary markets. Scenario 2 assumes substitution rates 10 percentage points lower, and scenario 3 assumes the substitution rates to be 20 percentage points lower than in the scenario 1.

Table 2.14. breaks down these sales losses by domestic market and exports. In 2013 UK IP right owners appeared to incur on average greater losses in export markets (GBP 4.9 billion) than in the UK itself (GBP 3.7 billion).

Table 2.14. Losses for UK IPR holders in domestic and export sales, 2013

Scenario 1

	Lost domestic sales		Lost exports	
Sector \ Unit	Value in GBP million	Share of domestic sales	Value in GBP million	Share of exports
Food, beverages and tobacco	723	2.35%	335	3.11%
Chemical and allied products	10	0.21%	80	1.71%
Pharmaceutical and medicinal chemical products	378	4.07%	1130	5.81%
Perfumery and cosmetics	208	5.35%	309	8.62%
Textiles and other intermediate products	479	3.40%	436	3.88%

Table 2.14. Losses for UK IPR holders in domestic and export sales, 2013

Scenario 1(continued)

	Lost domestic sales		Lost exports	
Sector \ Unit	Value in GBP million	Share of domestic sales	Value in GBP million	Share of exports
Clothing, footwear, leather and related products	67	4.33%	297	5.59%
Watches and jewellery	82	1.86%	690	1.24%
Non-metallic mineral products	39	1.42%	14	1.26%
Basic metals and fabricated metal products	63	0.51%	49	0.81%
Electrical household appliances, electronics, telecom.	366	1.78%	468	1.70%
Machinery; computers and peripheral equipment; ships and aircrafts	200	0.67%	394	1.09%
Motor vehicles and motorcycles	774	2.11%	463	1.55%
Household cultural and recreation goods	155	2.24%	126	3.58%
Furniture, lighting equipment and n.e.c	140	1.90%	18	0.99%
Total	**3682.9**	**1.99%**	**4916.7**	**1.91%**

Note: In scenario 1, a substitution rate of 39 % has been chosen for product category related to clothing and footwear, 49% for products related to the perfumery and cosmetics sector, 27% for products belonging to the watch and jewellery industries, and 32% for all other fake products sold on secondary markets.

What does counterfeiting mean for lost jobs in the UK manufacturing industry?

Lower sales of genuine UK-patented and trademarked products translates into fewer jobs in the affected UK manufacturing sectors. In order to estimate the amount of jobs lost due to infringement of Trademarks and patents of UK residents in global trade, the basic econometric model presented in Chapter 1 was used. This drew on the estimates of the transmission rates (elasticities) between lost sales and lost jobs (Table 1.3.).

Table 2.15. displays the total job losses in various branches of the UK manufacturing industry. **Overall, the total number of jobs lost in the UK industries due to infringement of UK-related IP-rights in global trade amounted to more than 20 000, equivalent to 1.29% of the total number of employees in the UK manufacturing sector.**

Table 2.15. Estimates of lost jobs in UK manufacturing industries, 2013

	Scenario 1		Scenario 2		Scenario 3	
Sector \ Unit	Number of employees	Share of employees	Number of employees	Share of employees	Number of employees	Share of employees
Food, beverages and tobacco	7413	2.48%	7409	2.47%	6887	2.30%
Chemical and allied products	53	0.13%	16	0.04%	9	0.02%
Pharmaceuticals	--	--	--	--	--	--
Perfumery and cosmetics	688	3.84%	582	3.25%	510	2.85%
Textiles and other intermediate products	4864	2.00%	3993	1.64%	3968	1.63%
Clothing, footwear, leather and related products	496	1.61%	422	1.37%	389	1.26%
Watches and jewellery	10	1.22%	8	0.92%	7	0.85%
Non-metallic mineral products	185	0.29%	198	0.31%	181	0.28%
Basic metals and fabricated metal products	836	0.18%	779	0.17%	666	0.15%
Electrical household appliances, electronics and telecommunications	2121	1.23%	1745	1.01%	1606	0.93%
Machinery, computers and peripheral equipment; ships and aircrafts	1933	0.50%	1689	0.44%	1575	0.41%
Motor vehicles and motorcycles	231	1.22%	211	1.11%	207	1.09%
Household cultural and recreation goods	12	1.10%	10	0.91%	8	0.73%
Furniture, lighting equipment and other manufacturing n.e.c	1397	1.04%	1298	0.96%	1272	0.94%
Total	**20239**	**1.29%**	**18361**	**1.17%**	**17285**	**1.10%**

Note: In scenario 1, a substitution rate of 39 % has been chosen for product category related to clothing and footwear, 49% for products related to the perfumery and cosmetics sector, 27% for products belonging to the watch and jewellery industries, and 32% for all other fake products sold on secondary markets. Scenario 2 assumes substitution rates 10 percentage points lower, and scenario 3 assumes the substitution rates to be 20 percentage points lower than in the scenario 1.

What do infringements of UK IPRs mean for government revenues?

Lower sales and lower profits for UK right holders mean they pay lower corporate income tax to the government. In addition, fewer employees mean lower personal income tax revenues and lower social security contributions. In 2013, this foregone tax revenue amounted to GBP 1.43 billion (Table 2.16.). The largest component was the foregone corporate income tax, amounting to GBP 630 million.

Table 2.16. Public revenue losses due to UK IPR-infringements in global trade, 2013

	Scenario 1	Scenario 2	Scenario 3
Social security contributions	338.8	308.3	284.1
Personal income taxes	458.1	455.9	454
Corporate taxes	630.3	627.2	624.6
Total	**1 427.2**	**1 391.3**	**1 362.7**
Share of governmental taxes	**0.34%**	**0.33%**	**0.32%**

Note: In scenario 1, a substitution rate of 39 % has been chosen for product category related to clothing and footwear, 49% for products related to the perfumery and cosmetics sector, 27% for products belonging to the watch and jewellery industries, and 32% for all other fake products sold on secondary markets. Scenario 2 assumes substitution rates 10 percentage points lower, and scenario 3 assumes the substitution rates to be 20 percentage points lower than in the scenario 1.

What is the impact on the UK overall?

This study has assessed quantitatively the value and scope of trade in counterfeit and pirated products in the UK context and gauged some of its impact on consumers, jobs, sales and tax revenue.

The previous two sections have quantified: (1) the impacts of imports of counterfeit and pirated products in the UK; and (2) the harmful effects of global trade in UK IPR-infringing products.

Adding together the results of these two investigations gives the overall impact of counterfeit trade on UK consumers, right holders and government.[2]

Concerning the total impact of counterfeit trade in the UK, the best available statistics show that the total consumer detriment due to consumer deception by counterfeiters in 2013 amounted to almost GBP 100 million. The sales losses to the UK wholesale and retail industries in 2013 amounted to GBP 4.22 billion, or 1.37% of total sales in that year. The total volume of foregone sales by the UK right owners due to infringement of their IP rights in 2013 amounted to GBP 8.6 billion pounds, or 1.95% of their total sales in that year. These sale losses translate in turn into lost jobs and lower tax returns (Table 2.17.).

Table 2.17. Total direct impact of counterfeit trade in the UK context (lost sales, jobs and taxes), 2013

Total lost sales (wholesale and retail)		Total lost sales (UK IP right owners)		Total lost jobs		Total lost taxes	
GBP 4.2 billion	1.37% of UK sales	GBP 8.6 billion	1.95% of UK firms' sales	60 334 jobs	1.15% of UK employment	GBP 3.8 billion	0.91% of governmental taxes

In particular, the best available estimates based on the customs data indicate that global counterfeiting and piracy in 2013 resulted in 60 thousand lost jobs in the UK, including 40 thousand in the retail and wholesale sector, and 20 thousand in the manufacturing sector.

For the same year, counterfeit trade resulted in almost 3 billion pounds of foregone tax revenue for the UK government, with 2 411 million due to counterfeit imports to the UK and 583 million due to illicit trade in goods that infringe IPR of UK residents.

Notes

1. Note that these data thus include customs seizures of both (1) counterfeit and pirated imports reported directly by the UK customs authorities; and (2) fake goods in transit to the UK in a third European country, and reported to DG TAXUD by other European customs officers.

2. Note that the methodology takes into account the "double-counting" issue which arises from the existence of imports of fake products to the UK that infringe the IPR of UK residents. This is done by breaking down the seizure dataset and identifying the economy of residence of rights holders whose IP rights were infringed. In addition, the framework looks only at areas where quantification was possible. The impact should definitely not be interpreted as the total impact of counterfeit trade in the UK.

References

Gallup Organisation (2007), *Global Consumer Awareness, Attitudes, and Opinions on Counterfeiting and Piracy*, The Gallup Organisation, Princeton.

OECD/EUIPO (2016), Trade in Counterfeit and Pirated Goods: Mapping the Economic Impact, OECD Publishing, Paris. DOI: http://dx.doi.org/10.1787/9789264252653-en.

Chapter 3.

Improving the evidence base on counterfeiting and piracy

This study has highlighted some important, data-related issues. These include a lack of compatibility and completeness of existing datasets and need for greater harmonisation of data collection; information gaps concerning consumer behaviour, especially on substitution rates; and difficulties in quantifying certain impacts of counterfeiting, e.g. the effects on consumers' health and safety.

Even though information on counterfeit and pirated trade has significantly improved in recent years, it still falls far short of what is needed for robust analysis and policy making. Further research on measurement techniques and data collection methods could help to refine the analysis and close the data gaps. The key data-related issues identified in this study refer to:

- Lack of compatibility and completeness of existing datasets, requiring greater harmonisation of data collection
- Information gaps on consumer behaviour, especially on substitution rates, requiring more surveys and experiments
- Difficulties in quantifying certain impacts of counterfeiting, e.g. the effects on consumers' health and safety, requiring more co-ordinated efforts

Lack of compatibility and completeness of existing datasets

The existing datasets and frameworks for data collection could be used more for improving our understanding of many aspects of counterfeiting and piracy. Unfortunately, as the analysis revealed, these datasets and the frameworks for data collection are often inconsistent or incomplete.

As different taxonomies have been used to create individual datasets which means they are often incompatible. Trying to match them can be very laborious or even impossible. For example, on the one hand datasets on counterfeit seizures were created from the trade-related taxonomies (Harmonized System), while data on industrial activity relies on the International Standard Industrial Classification of All Economic Activities (ISIC) categorisation. Matching these datasets could potentially provide a wealth of additional information, for example about the production points of counterfeit products. Unfortunately this matching is often impossible due to incompatibility between ISIC and HS taxonomies.

To address this issue more consistency is needed in data collection and harmonisation processes. For example the Customs Enforcement Network (CEN), a reporting framework developed by customs agencies through the World Customs Organization (WCO), offers one of the most promising ways forward for improving information on infringement of counterfeit and pirated products. The framework establishes the parameters for reporting on seized/intercepted products. The WCO's Harmonized System, for example, provides a coded nomenclature for over 5 200 items; using this, at the detailed six-digit level would provide much-needed specificity about the products being intercepted/seized.

At the same time numerous datasets turned out to be incomplete. For many years or categories the observations were simply missing. For example, even though the WCO noted that higher emphasis on the importance of CEN leads to a significant increase in the usage of the system, many countries are still inactive in reporting.

Information gaps concerning consumer behaviour

In addition to the further development and harmonization of existing datasets, far more can and should be done to improve understanding of consumer behaviour surrounding their purchase of counterfeit goods. This in particular refers to the estimation of substitution rates, which are critical when analysing the effects of counterfeiting and piracy on rights holders, but difficult to develop using traditional economic and econometric tools.

There are two general ways to assess the substitution rate: surveys and economic experiments. Irrespective of the method chosen, the assumptions underlying approaches should be clear, as should the economic arguments; transparency is key. Outcomes should be evaluated in terms of reasonableness and, wherever possible, be subject to sensitivity analysis to determine how variations in key assumptions affect outcomes.

Surveys are a potentially rich source for developing information on substitution rates. Their strength is that they can be designed to provide information on a very wide range of factors; both quantitative and qualitative, while allowing for numerous controls (e.g. gender, age and/or income). However, they are sensitive to the way questions are constructed and rely on the willingness of respondents to provide accurate responses – this could be a concern as respondents might be reluctant to report fully on unlawful behaviour. Surveys must therefore be well designed and targeted in a manner that provides information on the characteristics that are key to the analysis. A clearly defined and measurable research objective is thus critical. In addition, to enhance their value, surveys should be standardised as much as possible. This would facilitate cross-country and cross-sector analysis. Finally, repeating surveys periodically would provide opportunities for following developments over time.

Apart from surveys, economic experiments can also be used to gauge customers' substitution rates. An economic experiment can be seen as a combination of a classical survey and a laboratory experiment. The experimental part arises from the fact that the "survey" includes some form of incentive schemes designed to reveal the preferences and/or behavioural traits of participants. In relation to counterfeiting and piracy, such mechanisms can be useful for revealing how participants in the experiment value fake vs. genuine goods; the results can be used to help determine what consumers are willing to pay for different counterfeit and pirated items under different circumstances.

The experiments are performed under controlled laboratory conditions in a transparent and context-independent way. During an experiment participants are essentially tested to determine under what conditions they would buy a counterfeit/pirated product. The information developed through such experiments can be used to estimate or predict reactions to changes in demand for a genuine good under different rates of piracy.

Difficulties in quantifying certain impacts

There are several areas of counterfeiting and counterfeit trade for which no clear and commonly agreed methodology exists to gauge impacts. These include environmental harm due to the use of poor quality counterfeit chemicals, and adverse effects of counterfeits on consumers' health and safety.

There are numerous anecdotal reports on the adverse effects that counterfeit products can have on public health and safety or on the environment. The reports, however, have limited scope. A more systematic and extensive approach for developing data in this area is therefore needed. This has already highlighted in an OECD report on the economic impact of counterfeiting and piracy (OECD, 2008). The report presented a potential way of developing information on counterfeit medicine following Liang (2005). Under a "Patient Safety Reporting System", patients, medical practitioners and suppliers would provide inputs. Reporting would thereby not be restricted to professionals and rights holders, but would include consumers. To facilitate reporting, it was recommended that provisions be available for supplying input by email, the Internet (via web-based forms), mail or fax. While the focus of the system was directed exclusively towards pharmaceuticals, it could be adapted for use more widely.

Another idea advanced by Forzley (2003) would be to build a better platform for general data development by providing a means for registering infringement-inflicted harm to consumers under public health disease classifications of unintentional injury. The first step in this direction would involve the introduction of codes for harm caused by counterfeit articles in the International Classification of Diseases (ICD). This should be followed by improvement of systems used to develop and monitor statistics on health and safety concerning transportation, food, drinks, drugs, and consumer products. These systems should register the infringement-inflicted accidents, injuries and deaths.

Some progress is being made on collecting data on effects in a more systematic fashion, particularly in the pharmaceuticals sector. An International Medical Products Anti-Counterfeiting Taskforce (IMPACT)[1] was recently created by the World Health Organization (WHO), which, among other things, has the goal of developing accessible and reliable information on the nature and extent of the problem. The taskforce has simplified the process and tools for reporting counterfeit medicine, and data collection is now facilitated by the Rapid Alert System (RAS)[2] which is a web-based reporting platform accessible to any interested party.

Despite these sectoral initiatives introduced over ten years ago, the methodological gap is still large. More co-ordinated effort is needed to develop frameworks to gauge these important harmful effects of counterfeiting on health, safety and the environment.

Notes

1. WHO (World Health Organization) (2017), Substandard, spurious, falsely labelled, falsified and counterfeit (SSFFC) medical products web page, http://www.who.int/medicines/regulation/ssffc/en (accessed 11 April 2017).

2. European Commission (2017), Rapid Alert System for dangerous non-food products web page, http://ec.europa.eu/consumers/consumers_safety/safety_products/rapex/alerts/repository/content/pages/rapex/index_en.htm (accessed 19 June 2017).

References

OECD (2008), *The Economic Impact of Counterfeiting and Piracy*, OECD Publishing, Paris, http://dx.doi.org/10.1787/9789264045521-en.

Forzley, M. (2003), *Counterfeit Goods and the Public's Health and Safety*, International Intellectual Property Institute.

Liang, B. (2005), "Measuring the Impact of Counterfeit Drugs: Applying the Patient Safety Reporting System Approach", presentation at OECD/WIPO meeting on measurement of counterfeiting and piracy, 17-18 October.

Chapter 4.

Conclusions and next steps

The findings of this study should help both public and private sector decision makers to better understand the nature and scale of the trade in counterfeit goods for the UK economy, and to develop appropriate, cohesive, and evidence-based policy responses. Furthermore, the methodology developed for this report can lend itself to a number of additional exercises. These could include other country studies, which could eventually lead to a benchmarking exercise. This methodology could be also re-used to determine the scale of harm caused by counterfeiting on the UK economy once the new data become available.

This report has presented a state-of-the-art quantitative analysis of the scale of counterfeiting in the UK context and of its negative impacts in certain areas, such as on jobs, consumers and public revenue. The study developed a methodology to gauge the magnitude and scale of counterfeit trade in the UK and to quantify its direct economic impact. It relied primarily on a unique international set of customs seizure data, as well as structured interviews with trade and customs experts.

The results show that imports of counterfeit goods to the UK accounted for as much as GBP 9 billion in 2013. This represents 4% of UK imports, well above the 2.5% average share of fake goods in world imports. In the same year global trade in products that infringe UK trademarks or patents accounted for as much as GBP 1.4 billion. This represents 3% of the UK manufacturing production. China is the main provenance country for both counterfeit goods traded to the UK, and counterfeit goods that infringe IP rights of UK firms.

In addition to quantifying the magnitude and scale of counterfeit trade in the UK, the study also estimated its direct, economic effects on the UK. In particular, the best available estimates based on the customs data indicate that global counterfeiting and piracy in 2013 resulted in 60 000 lost jobs in the UK, comprising 40 000 in the retail and wholesale sector, and 20 000 in the manufacturing sector. That same year, counterfeit and pirated trade resulted in almost GBP 3.8 billion of foregone tax revenue for the UK government, of which GBP 2.4 billion were due to counterfeit imports to the UK and 1.4 billion were due to illicit trade in goods that infringe IPR of UK residents.

The magnitude of the issue, and the scale of its impact, should be of concern to both policy makers and the private sector. It has significant implications for the future, including on the UK's highest added value activities and innovation potential, both of which are sources of long-term economic growth.

Next steps

The unique methodology developed for this report can lend itself to a number of additional exercises. These could include other country studies, which could eventually lead to a benchmarking exercise. The potential for additional case studies is particularly fruitful where the data are abundant and where there is evidence of significant impact by infringements.

The methodology could also be successfully and repetitively re-applied to determine the relative changes of the scale and impacts of counterfeiting and piracy in the UK. In addition, the methodology offers some flexibility to accommodate improvements in research, for on example substitution rates. This could lead to a more detailed analysis that would produce a more complete picture of trade in counterfeit and pirated goods, and its negative impact on right holders, governments and consumers in the UK. Chapter 3 points to a number of areas where methodologies and data collection can be improved.

Annex A. Methodological appendix

Annex A.1. Construction of the GTRIC for imports

Construction of GTRIC-p

GTRIC-p is constructed through three steps:

1. For each product category, the seizure percentages for sensitive goods are formed.
2. From these, a counterfeit a source factor is established for each industry, based on the industries' weight in terms of UK total imports.
3. Based on these factors, the GTRIC-p is formed.

Step 1: Measuring product seizure intensities

v_p and m_p are, respectively, the seizure and import values of product type p (as registered according to the HS on the two-digit level) shipped to the UK from *any* provenance economy in a given year. The relative seizure intensity (seizure percentages) of good p, denoted below as γ_p, is then defined by:

$$\gamma_p = \frac{v_p}{\sum_p v_p}, \text{ such that } \sum_p \gamma_p = 1$$

Step 2: Measuring product-specific counterfeiting factors

$M = \sum_p m_p$ is defined as the total registered imports by the UK of all sensitive goods.

The import share of good p, denoted s_p, is therefore given by:

$$s_p = \frac{m_p}{M}, \text{ such that } \sum_p s_p = 1$$

The counterfeiting factor of product category p, denoted C_p, is then determined as the following.

$$C_p = \frac{\gamma_p}{s_p}$$

The counterfeiting factor reflects the sensitivity of product infringements occurring in a particular product category, relative to its share in UK imports. These constitute the foundation of the formation of GTRIC-p.

Step 3: Establishing GTRIC-p

GTRIC-p is constructed from a transformation of the counterfeiting factor and measures the relative propensity to which different types of product categories are subject to counterfeiting and piracy in UK imports. The transformation of the counterfeiting factor is based on two main assumptions:

1. The first assumption (A1) is that the counterfeiting factor of a particular product category is positively correlated with the actual intensity of trade in counterfeit and pirated goods covered by that chapter. The counterfeiting factors must thus reflect the real intensity of actual counterfeit trade in the given product categories.

2. The second assumption (A2) acknowledges that the assumption may not be entirely correct. For instance, the fact that infringing goods are detected more frequently in certain categories could imply that differences in counterfeiting factors across products merely reflect that some goods are easier to detect than others, or that some goods, for one reason or another, have been specially targeted for inspection. The counterfeiting factors of product categories with lower counterfeiting factors could therefore underestimate actual counterfeiting and piracy intensities in these cases.

In accordance with assumption A1 (positive correlation between counterfeiting factors and actual infringement activities) and assumption A2 (lower counterfeiting factors may underestimate actual activities), GTRIC-p is established by applying a positive monotonic transformation of the counterfeiting factor index using natural logarithms. This standard technique of linearisation of a non-linear relationship (in the case of this study between counterfeiting factors and actual infringement activities) allows the index to be flattened and gives a higher relative weight to lower counterfeiting factors (see Verbeek, 2000)

In order to address the possibility of outliers in both ends of the counterfeiting factor index; i.e. some categories may be measured as particularly susceptible to infringement even though they are not, whereas others may be measured as insusceptible although they are; it is assumed that GTRIC-p follows a left-truncated normal distribution, with GTRIC-p only taking values of zero or above.

The transformed counterfeiting factor is defined as:

$$c_p = \ln(C_p + 1)$$

Assuming that the transformed counterfeiting factor can be described by a left-truncated normal distribution with $c_p \geq 0$; then, following Hald (1952), the density function of GTRIC-p is given by:

$$f_{LTN}(c_p) = \begin{cases} 0 & if\, cf_p \leq 0 \\ \dfrac{f(c_p)}{\int_0^{\infty} f(c_p)\, dc_p} & if\, cf_p \geq 0 \end{cases}$$

where $f(c_p)$ is the non-truncated normal distribution for c_p specified as:

$$f(c_p) = \frac{1}{\sqrt{2\pi\sigma_p^2}} \exp\left(-\frac{1}{2}\left(\frac{c_p - \mu_p}{\sigma_p}\right)^2\right)$$

The mean and variance of the normal distribution, here denoted μ_p and σ_p^2 , are estimated over the transformed counterfeiting factor index, c_p, and given by $\hat{\mu}_p$ and $\hat{\sigma}_p^2$. This enables the calculation of the counterfeit import propensity index (GTRIC-p) across HS chapters, corresponding to the cumulative distribution function of c_p.

Construction of GTRIC-e

GTRIC-e is also constructed in three steps:

1. For each provenance economy, the seizure percentages are calculated.
2. From these, each provenance economy's counterfeit source factor is established, based on the provenance economies' weight in terms of UK total imports.
3. Based on these factors, the GTRIC-e is formed.

Step 1: Measuring seizure intensities from each provenance economy

v_e is UK's registered seizures of all types of infringing goods (i.e. all p) originating from economy e at a given year in terms of their value.

γ_e is UK's relative seizure intensity (seizure percentage) of all infringing items that originate from economy e, in a given year:

$$\gamma_e = \frac{v_e}{\sum_e v_e}, \text{ such that } \sum_e \gamma_e = 1$$

Step 2: Measuring partner-specific counterfeiting factors

m_e is defined as the total registered UK imports of all sensitive products from e, and $M = \sum_e m_e$ is the total UK import of sensitive goods from all provenance economies.

The share of imports from provenance economy e in total UK imports of sensitive goods, denoted s_e, is then given by:

$$s_e = \frac{m_e}{M}, \text{ such that } \sum_e s_e = 1$$

From this, the economy-specific counterfeiting factor is established by dividing the general seizure intensity for economy e with the share of total imports of sensitive goods from e.

$$C_e = \frac{\gamma_e}{s_e}$$

Step 3: Establishing GTRIC-e

Gauging the magnitude of counterfeiting and piracy from a provenance economy perspective can be undertaken in a similar fashion as for sensitive goods. Hence, a general trade-related index of counterfeiting for economies (GTRIC-e) is established along similar lines and assumptions:

1. The first assumption (A3) is that the intensity by which any counterfeit or pirated article from a particular economy is detected and seized by customs is positively correlated with the actual amount of counterfeit and pirate articles imported from that location.
2. The second assumption (A4) acknowledges that assumption A3 may not be entirely correct. For instance, a high seizure intensity of counterfeit or pirated articles from a particular provenance

economy could be an indication that the provenance economy is part of a customs profiling scheme, or that it is specially targeted for investigation by customs. The importance that provenance economies with low seizure intensities play regarding actual counterfeiting and piracy activity could therefore be under-represented by the index and lead to an underestimation of the scale of counterfeiting and piracy.

As with the product-specific index, GTRIC-e is established by applying a positive monotonic transformation of the counterfeiting factor index for provenance economies using natural logarithms. This follows from assumption A3 (positive correlation between seizure intensities and actual infringement activities) and assumption A4 (lower intensities tend to underestimate actual activities). Considering the possibilities of outliers at both ends of the GTRIC-e distribution; i.e. some economies may be wrongly measured as being particularly susceptible sources of counterfeit and pirated imports, and vice versa; GTRIC-e is approximated by a left-truncated normal distribution as it does not take values below zero.

The transformed general counterfeiting factor across provenance economies on which GTRIC-e is based is therefore given by applying logarithms onto economy-specific general counterfeit factors (see, for example, Verbeek, 2000):

$$c_e = \ln(C_e + 1)$$

In addition, following GTRIC-p it is assumed that GTRIC-e follows a truncated normal distribution with $c_e \geq 0$ for all e. Following Hald (1952), the density function of the left-truncated normal distribution for c_e is given by

$$g(c_p) = \begin{cases} 0 & if\,cf_e \leq 0 \\ \dfrac{g(e)}{\int_0^\infty g(c_e)\,dc_e} & if\,cf_e \geq 0 \end{cases}$$

where $g(cf_e)$ is the non-truncated normal distribution for c_e specified as:

$$g(c_e) = \frac{1}{\sqrt{2\pi\sigma_e^2}} \exp\left(-\frac{1}{2}\left(\frac{c_e - \mu_e}{\sigma_e}\right)^2\right)$$

The mean and variance of the normal distribution, here denoted μ_e and σ_e^2, are estimated over the transformed counterfeiting factor index, c_e, and given by $\hat{\mu}_e$ and $\hat{\sigma}_e^2$.. This enables the calculation of the counterfeit import propensity index (GTRIC-e) across provenance economies, corresponding to the cumulative distribution function ofc_e.

Construction of GTRIC

The combined index of GTRIC-e and GTRIC-p, denoted GTRIC, is an index that approximates the relative propensities to which particular product types, imported by the UK from specific trading partners, are counterfeit and/or pirated.

Step 1: Establishing propensities for product and provenance economy

In this step the propensities to contain counterfeit and pirated products will be established for each trade flow from a given provenance economy and in a given product category.

The general propensity of importing infringed items of HS category p, from any economy, is denoted P_p and be given by GTRIC-p so that:

$$P_p = F_{LTN}(c_p)$$

where $F_{LTN}(c_p)$ is the cumulative probability function of $f_{LTN}(c_p)$.

Furthermore, the general propensity of importing any type of infringing goods from economy e is denoted P_e, and given by GTRIC-e, so that:

$$P_e = G_{LTN}(c_e)$$

where $G_{LTN}(c_e)$ is the cumulative probability function of $g_{LTN}(c_e)$.

The general propensity of importing counterfeit or pirated items of type p originating from economy $e$is then denoted P_{ep} and approximated by:

$$P_{ep} = P_p P_e$$

Therefore, $P_{ep} \in \left[\varepsilon_p \varepsilon_e\ ; 1\right]$, $\forall e, p$, with $\varepsilon_p \varepsilon_e$ denoting the minimum average counterfeit export rate for each sensitive product category and each provenance economy.[16] It is assumed that $\varepsilon_e = \varepsilon_p = 0.05$.

Step 2: Calculating the absolute value

α is the fixed point, i.e. the maximum average counterfeit import rate of a given type of infringing good, p, originating from a given trading partner, e. α can therefore be applied onto propensities of importing infringing goods of type p from trading partner e (αP^{jk}).

As a result, a matrix of counterfeit import propensities $\boldsymbol{C}$ is obtained.

$$\boldsymbol{C} = \begin{pmatrix} \alpha P_{11} & \alpha P_{12} & & & \alpha P_{1P} \\ \alpha P_{21} & \ddots & & & \\ & & \alpha P_{ep} & & \\ & & & \ddots & \\ \alpha P_{E1} & & & & \alpha P_{EP} \end{pmatrix} \text{ with dimension } E \times P$$

The matrix of UK imports is denoted by $\boldsymbol{M}$**.** Applying $\boldsymbol{C}$ on $\boldsymbol{M}$ yields the absolute volume of imports of counterfeit and pirated goods to the UK. In particular, the import matrix $\boldsymbol{M}$ is given by:

$$\boldsymbol{M} = \begin{pmatrix} m_{11} & m_{12} & & & m_{1P} \\ m_{21} & \ddots & & & \\ & & m_{ep} & & \\ & & & \ddots & \\ m_{E1} & & & & \alpha m_{EP} \end{pmatrix} \text{ with dimension } E \times P$$

Hence, the element m_{ep} denotes UK's imports of product category p from trading partner e, with $e = [1, \dots, E]$ and $p = [1, \dots, P]$.

Denoted by $\boldsymbol{\Psi}$, the product-by-economy percentage of counterfeit and pirated imports can be determined as the following:

$$\mathbf{\Psi} = \mathbf{C}'\mathbf{M} \div \mathbf{M}$$

Total imports in counterfeit and pirated goods, denoted by the scalar $\boldsymbol{TC}$, is then given by:

$$\mathbf{TC} = \mathbf{I_1}'\mathbf{\Psi}\mathbf{I_2}$$

where $\mathbf{I_1}$ is a vector of one with dimension $E \times 1$, and $\mathbf{I_2}$ is a vector of one with dimension $P \times 1$.

Then, by denoting total world trade by the scalar $\mathbf{TM} = \mathbf{I_1}\mathbf{M}'\mathbf{I_2}$, the value of counterfeiting and piracy in UK imports, $\boldsymbol{S_{TC}}$, is determined by:

$$\boldsymbol{S_{TC}} = \frac{\boldsymbol{TC}}{\boldsymbol{TM}}$$

Annex A.2. Construction of the GTRIC for products infringing UK IPRs

Construction of UK-GTRIC-p

UK-GTRIC-p is constructed of three steps:

1. For each product category, the seizure percentages for sensitive goods are formed.
2. From these, a counterfeit a source factor is established for each industry, based on the industries' weight in terms of total trade.
3. Based on these factors, the GTRIC-p is formed.

Step 1: Measuring product seizure intensities

w_p is the seized value of product type p (as registered according to the HS on the two-digit level) infringing UK residents' IP rights from any provenance economy in a given year. The relative seizure intensity (seizure percentages) of good p, denoted below as η_p, is then defined by:

$$\eta_p = \frac{w_p}{\sum_p w_p}, \text{ such that } \sum\nolimits_p \eta_p = 1$$

Step 2: Measuring product-specific counterfeiting factors

x_p is the total sales value (exports plus domestic sales) of product of type p, so that $X = \sum_p x_p$ is defined as the total registered sales by the UK industries of all sensitive goods.

The share of good k in UK total sales, denoted ς_p, is therefore given by:

$$\varsigma_p = \frac{x_p}{X}, \text{such that} \sum\nolimits_p \varsigma_p = 1$$

The counterfeiting factor of product category p, denoted F_p, is then determined as the following.

$$F_p = \frac{\eta_p}{\varsigma_p}$$

The counterfeiting factor reflects the sensitivity of infringements of Trademarks and patents of UK residents occurring in a particular product category, relative to its share in UK total sales. These constitute the foundation of the formation of GTRIC-p.

Step 3: Establishing GTRIC-p

GTRIC-p is constructed from a transformation of the counterfeiting factor and measures the relative propensity to which Trademarks and patents of UK residents in different types of product categories are subject to counterfeiting and piracy. The transformation of the counterfeiting factor is based on two main assumptions:

In accordance with assumption A1 (positive correlation between counterfeiting factors and actual infringement activities) and assumption A2 (lower counterfeiting factors may underestimate actual activities) specified in Annex A.1, GTRIC-p is established by applying a positive monotonic transformation of the counterfeiting factor index using natural logarithms. This standard technique of linearisation of a non-linear relationship (in the case of this study between counterfeiting factors and actual infringement activities) allows the index to be flattened and gives a higher relative weight to lower counterfeiting factors (see Verbeek, 2000)

In addition, in order to address the possibility of outliers in both ends of the counterfeiting factor index; i.e. some categories may be measured as particularly susceptible to infringement even though they are not, whereas others may be measured as insusceptible although they are; it is assumed that GTRIC-p follows a left-truncated normal distribution, with GTRIC-p only taking values of zero or above.

The transformed counterfeiting factor is defined as:

$$f_p = \ln(F_p + 1)$$

Assuming that the transformed counterfeiting factor can be described by a left-truncated normal distribution with $f_p \geq 0$; then, following Hald (1952), the density function of GTRIC-p is given by:

$$h_{LTN}(f_p) = \begin{cases} 0 & if\, f_p \leq 0 \\ \dfrac{h(f_p)}{\int_0^{\infty} h(f_p)\, df_p} & if\, f_p \geq 0 \end{cases}$$

where $h(f_p)$ is the non-truncated normal distribution for cf_p specified as:

$$h(f_p) = \frac{1}{\sqrt{2\pi\sigma_p^2}} \exp\left(-\frac{1}{2}\left(\frac{f_p - \mu_p}{\sigma_p}\right)^2\right)$$

The mean and variance of the normal distribution, here denoted μ_p and σ_p^2 , are estimated over the transformed counterfeiting factor index, f_p, and given by $\hat{\mu}_p$ and $\hat{\sigma}_p^2$. This enables the calculation of the counterfeit propensity index (GTRIC-p) across HS chapters, corresponding to the cumulative distribution function of f_p.

Construction of UK-GTRIC-e

GTRIC-e is also constructed in three steps:

1. For each provenance economy, the seizure percentages are calculated.
2. From these, each provenance economy's counterfeit source factor is established, based on the provenance economies' weight in terms of UK total sales.
3. Based on these factors, the GTRIC-e is formed.

Step 1: Measuring seizure intensities to each destination economy

w_e is the registered seized value of all types of goods infringing Bristish residents'IP rights (i.e. all p) exported to economy e from any provenance economy at a given year. η_e is the relative seizure intensity (seizure percentage) of all products infringing Trademarks and patents of UK residents that are shipped to country e, in a given year:

$$\eta_e = \frac{w_e}{\sum_e w_e}, \text{ such that } \sum_e \eta_e = 1$$

Step 2: Measuring destination-specific counterfeiting factors

x_e is defined as the total registered UK sales value (exports plus domestic sales) of all sensitive products shipped to e and X is the total UK sales value of sensitive goods to all destination economies.

The share of sales to destination economy e in UK total sales of sensitive goods, denoted ς_e, is then given by:

$$\varsigma_e = \frac{x_e}{X}, \text{ such that } \sum_e \varsigma_e = 1$$

From this, the economy-specific counterfeiting factor is established by dividing the seizure intensity for economy d with the share of total sales of sensitive goods to e.

$$F_e = \frac{\eta_e}{\varsigma_e}$$

Step 3: Establishing GTRIC-e

Gauging the magnitude of counterfeiting and piracy targeting Trademarks and patents of UK residents in a given destination economy can be undertaken in a similar fashion as for Annex A.1. Thus, a general trade-related index of counterfeiting for economies (GTRIC-e) is established along similar lines and assumptions than A3 and A4 specified in Annex A.1.

The transformed general counterfeiting factor across destination economies on which GTRIC-e is based is therefore given by applying logarithms onto economy-specific general counterfeit factors (see, for example, Verbeek, 2000):

$$f_e = \ln(F_e + 1)$$

In addition, following GTRIC-p it is assumed that GTRIC-e follows a truncated normal distribution with $f_e \geq 0$ for all j. Following Hald

(1952), the density function of the left-truncated normal distribution for $f_e \geq 0$ is given by

$$i_{LTN}(f_e) = \begin{cases} 0 & if f_e \leq 0 \\ \dfrac{i(f_e)}{\int_0^{\infty} i(f_e)\, df_e} & if f_e \geq 0 \end{cases}$$

where $i(f_e)$ is the non-truncated normal distribution for f_e specified as:

$$i(f_e) = \frac{1}{\sqrt{2\pi\sigma_e^2}} \exp\left(-\frac{1}{2}\left(\frac{f_e - \mu_e}{e}\right)^2\right)$$

The mean and variance of the normal distribution, here denoted μ_e and σ_e^2, are estimated over the transformed counterfeiting factor index, f_e, and given by $\hat{\mu}_e$ and $\hat{\sigma}_e^2$. This enables the calculation of the counterfeit import propensity index (GTRIC-e) across provenance economies, corresponding to the cumulative distribution function of f_e.

Construction of UK-GTRIC

The combined index of GTRIC-e and GTRIC-p, denoted GTRIC, is an index that approximates the relative propensities for goods associated with UK residents' IP rights in a given product category and a given destination economy to be counterfeit and/or pirated.

Step 1: Establishing propensities for product and destination economy

The general propensity for Trademarks and patents of UK residents to be counterfeit or pirated in HS category p, is denoted Q_p, and is given by GTRIC-p so that:

$$Q_p = H_{LTN}(f_p)$$

where $H_{LTN}(f_p)$ is the cumulative probability function of $h_{LTN}(f_p)$.

Furthermore, the general propensity for all Trademarks and patents of UK residents to be infringed and shipped to economy e is denoted Q_e, and is given by GTRIC-e, so that:

$$Q_e = I_{LTN}(f_e)$$

where $I_{LTN}(cf_e)$ is the cumulative probability function of $i_{LTN}(cf_e)$.

The general propensity for UK residents' IP rights to be counterfeit or pirated in a given product category p and to be shipped to a given destination e from any provenance economy is then denoted Q_{ep} and approximated by:

$$Q_{ep} = Q_e Q_p$$

Therefore, $Q_{ep} \in [\nu_p \nu_e \,;\, 1]$, $\forall e, p$, with $\nu_p \nu_e$ denoting the minimum average counterfeit export rate for each sensitive product category and each destination economy. It is assumed that $\nu_p = \nu_e = 0.05$.

Step 2: Calculating the absolute value

β is the fixed point, i.e. the maximum average counterfeit rate of Trademarks and patents of UK residents for a given product type p, shipped to a given trading partner, e. β can therefore be applied onto propensities for UK-related IP rights of type p to be counterfeit and shipped to destination partner e (βQ_{ep}).

As a result, a matrix of propensities of counterfeiting F is obtained.

$$F = \begin{pmatrix} \beta Q_{11} & \beta Q_{12} & & & \beta Q_{1P} \\ \beta Q_{21} & \ddots & & & \\ & & \beta Q_{ep} & & \\ & & & \ddots & \\ \beta Q_{E1} & & & & \beta Q_{EP} \end{pmatrix} \text{ with dimension } E \times P$$

The matrix of UK total sales is denoted by X. Applying C on X yields the absolute volume of counterfeit and pirated trade in products that infringe UK residents' IP. In particular, the sales matrix X is given by:

$$X = \begin{pmatrix} \beta x_{11} & \beta x_{12} & & & \beta x_{1P} \\ \beta x_{21} & \ddots & & & \\ & & \beta x_{ep} & & \\ & & & \ddots & \\ \beta x_{E1} & & & & \beta x_{EP} \end{pmatrix} \text{ with dimension } E \times P$$

Hence, the element x_{ep} denotes UK's sales of products in category p to destination e, including the UK (i.e. domestic sales), with $e = [1, \dots, E]$ and $p = [1, \dots, P]$.

Denoted by Ω, the product-by-economy percentage of counterfeit and pirated imports can be determined as the following:

$$\Omega = \mathrm{F}'\mathrm{X} \div \mathrm{X}$$

Total trade in counterfeit and pirated goods that infringe British trademarks and patents, denoted by the scalar TF, is then given by:

$$\mathrm{TF} = I_1{}'\Omega\, I_2$$

where I_1 is a vector of one with dimension $E \times 1$, and I_2 is a vector of one with dimension $P \times 1$.

Then, by denoting total UK sales by the scalar $\mathrm{TX} = I_1{}'\mathrm{X}\, I_2$, the value of counterfeiting and piracy targeting UK residents' IP rights, ω_{TF}, is determined by:

$$\omega_{TF} = \frac{TF}{TX}$$

Annex A.3. Model to estimate transmission rates between lost sales and lost jobs

Existing economic literature does not determine clear the values of transmission between lost sales and lost jobs for each industry. Consequently, this study develops a simple econometric model to address this issue.

The idea behind the model is to invert a basic production function in a partial equilibrium model in order to estimate the response of employment to a shock on sales. Let $\hat{p}_p$ and $\hat{Q}_P$ denote, respectively, the average unit price and the total production in volume of (genuine) goods in industry p, so that the total sales of (genuine) goods in an industry is defined by

$$\hat{S}_p = \hat{p}_p \times \hat{Q}_P$$

The goods in the industry are produced using labor, $\hat{L}_p$, capital $\hat{K}_p$, and intermediate inputs $\hat{I}_p$, following a Cobb-Douglas production:

$$\hat{Q}_P = A_p\, \hat{L}_p^{\alpha}\, \hat{K}_p^{\beta}\, \hat{I}_p^{\gamma}$$

with A_p the total factor productivity (TFP). In accordance with the traditional economic literature, the firms' profit maximization problem within an industry yield an optimal price which equalizes a markup φ_p, over a marginal cost, here the productivity-adjusted wage w_p :

$$\hat{p}_p = \varphi_p \, w_p$$

Combining equations (1), (2), and (3), and taking the log yields:

$$\ln(\hat{S}_p) = \ln(\varphi_p) + \ln(w_p) + \ln(A_p) + \alpha \ln(\hat{L}_p) + \beta \ln(\hat{K}_p) + \gamma \ln(\hat{I}_p)$$

By inverting equation (4), employment can be expressed as a function of the other variables, including sales. Adding the subscripts $t$for a given year, as well as (i) year-fixed effects, δ_t, to account for common macroeconomic shocks across industries; and (ii) industry-fixed effects, δ_p, to account for the level of mark-up – which depends on the competition within the industry, the price elasticity of demand etc. – and the TFP – which may be considered as constant in the short-run (i.e. in the case of this study three years) – the following econometric specification is obtained:

$$\ln(\hat{L}_{pt}) = \beta_0 + \delta_t + \delta_p + \beta_1 \ln(\hat{K}_{pt}) + \beta_2 \ln(\hat{I}_{pt}) + \beta_3 \ln(\hat{S}_{pt}) + \sum_p \beta_p [\ln(\hat{S}_{pt}) \times \delta_p] + \varepsilon_{pt}$$

with β_0 a constant and ε_{pt} the error term. The estimates of the elasticity of employment with respect to sales for each industry can then be extracted from equation (5), and are given by $\xi_p = \beta_3 + \beta_p$. An estimated elasticity of ξ_p% means that a decrease of 1% in sales is translated into a decrease of ξ_p% in jobs.

The results of the econometric specification (5) for the UK retail and wholesale sector are displayed in Table A.1. below. The first column shows the coefficients estimated without the inclusion of industry fixed-effects, and indicates that an increase in 1% of sales in the retail and wholesale sector implies on average a 0.46% increase of the number of employees within the sector. The second column of Table A.1 adds cross effects between the logarithm of sales and the industry fixed-effects to the econometric specification, which leads to the industry-specific estimates of the elasticity of employment with respect to sales displayed in Table 1.2. of Step 5.

Table A.1. Estimation of sales elasticity of employment, UK wholesale and retail sector

Dependent variable: log employment		
log Capital	0.052	0.066
	(-0.044)	(-0.045)
log Intermediate Inputs	-0.134*	-0.112*
	(-0.071)	(-0.071)
log Productivity	-0.125***	-0.141***
	(-0.021)	(-0.023)
log Wages	-0.146***	-0.134***
	(-0.028)	(-0.029)
log Sales	0.465***	0.532***
	(-0.07)	(-0.072)
_cons	6.039*	5.067***
	(-0.531)	(-0.509)
Industry fixed-effects	Yes	Yes
Year fixed-effects	Yes	Yes
Cross log Sales x Industry fixed-effects	No	Yes
Adjusted R^2	0.871	0.882
Number of observations	45	45

Notes: Standard errors in parentheses. * p<0.05; ** p<0.01; *** p<0.001. The industrial data for UK industries over the period 2009-2014 are provided by Eurostat. Employment is measure by the number of full-time equivalent employees; capital by the gross investment in intangible goods; intermediate inputs by total purchases of goods and services; sales by turnovers; wages by the ratio of total personal costs, including social security costs, to the number of full-time equivalent employees; productivity by labour productivity.

The above present model can be used to perform a similar exercise for the UK manufacturing industries. The results of this estimation are displayed in Table A.2. below. The first column indicates that the transmission rate between changes in sales and changes in the level of employment is on average slightly lower than for the UK retail and whole industries, with an average estimate of 0.43%. Once again, the second column of Table A.2 adds cross effects between industry fixed-effects and the logarithm of sales, which give us the industry-specific estimates of the elasticity of the number of employees with respect to sales that are displayed in Table 1.3. of Step 10.

Table A.2. Estimation of sales elasticity of jobs, UK manufacturing sector

Dependent variable: log employment		
log Capital	0.066***	0.078***
	(-0.017)	(-0.017)
log Intermediate Inputs	-0.071	-0.081
	(-0.073)	(-0.076)
log Productivity	-0.325***	-0.341***
	(-0.044)	(-0.047)
log Wages	-0.945***	-0.949***
	(-0.016)	(-0.017)
log Sales	0.426***	0.643***
	(-0.084)	(-0.086)
_cons	5.281***	4.398***
	(-0.307)	(-0.315)
Industry fixed-effects	Yes	Yes
Year fixed-effects	Yes	Yes
Cross log Sales x Industry fixed-effects	No	Yes
Adjusted R2	0.915	0.925
Number of observations	256	256

Notes: Standard errors in parentheses. * $p<0.05$; ** $p<0.01$; *** $p<0.001$. The industrial data for UK industries over the period 2009-2014 are provided by Eurostat. Employment is measure by the number of full-time equivalent employees; capital by the gross investment in intangible goods; intermediate inputs by total purchases of goods and services; sales by turnovers; wages by the ratio of total personal costs, including social security costs, to the number of full-time equivalent employees; productivity by labour productivity.

Annex A.4. Examples of primary and secondary markets identifications

Specific examples for counterfeit and pirated imports to the UK territory

Example 1

This example considers boots of a brand that is the most frequently seized item in the UK. Figure 1 displayed in the second Step of Part 1 shows the unit price distribution of all boots of that brad that were seized by UK customs authorities between 2011 and 2013.

The identification of primary and secondary market using the methodology described in Step 2 implies that seized shipments of these boots associated with unit values strictly lower than GBP 165 are classified into the secondary market, whereas those associated with unit values larger than GBP 165 are classified into the primary market. This leads to the following results:

Table A.3. Share of the primary and secondary markets for counterfeit boots of the analysed brand, 2011-2013

	Freq.	Percent
Primary market	10,902	43.76
Secondary market	14,013	56.24
Total	**24,915**	**100.00**

In words, 56% of the analysed boots shipments seized by UK customs between 2011 and 2013 were intended to be sold in the primary market and the rest of them in the secondary market.

Example 2

Shoes of the analysed brand are the second most frequently seized item in the UK. Figure A.1 below shows the price distribution of counterfeit shoes of the analysed brand exported to the UK territory and that were seized by UK customs authorities between 2011 and 2013:

Figure A.1. Price distribution of counterfeit shoes of the analysed brand seized by UK customs, 2011-2013

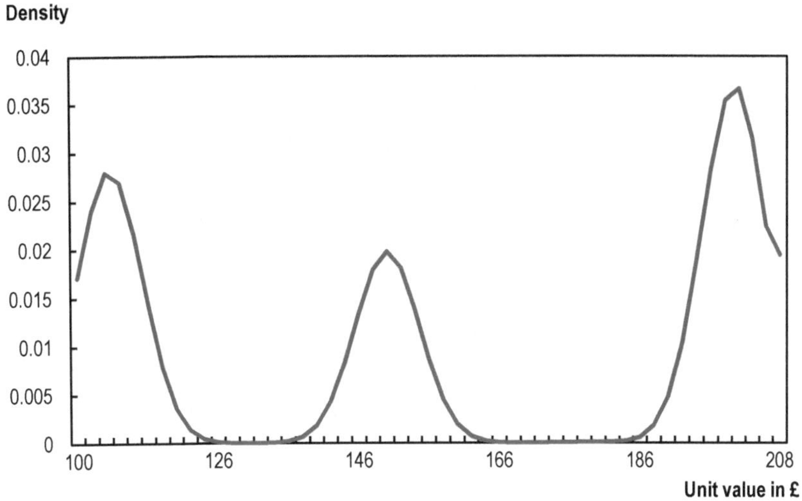

StatLink http://dx.doi.org/10.1787/888933553252

The identification of primary and secondary markets using the methodology described in Step 2 implies that seized shipments of shoes of the analysed brand associated unit values strictly lower than GBP 100 are classified into the secondary market, whereas those associated with unit values larger than GBP 100 are classified into the primary market. This leads to the following results:

Table A.4. Share of the primary and secondary markets for counterfeit shoes of the analysed brand seized by UK customs, 2011-2013

	Freq.	Percent
Primary market	3,496	54,50
Secondary market	2,919	45,50
Total	**6,415**	**100**

In words, 54.5% of shipments of shoes of the analysed brand seized by UK customs authorities between 2011 and 2013 were intended to be sold in the primary market and the rest of them in the secondary market.

Specific examples for counterfeit and pirated products traded worldwide that infringe UK trademarks

Example 3

The electrical product of a given brand registered by a UK company (H 85) is the most popular UK product seized worldwide. Figure A.2. Price distribution of counterfeit electrical products of a given brand seized by customs authorities worldwide, 2011-2013below reports the price distribution of these products that were seized by customs authorities worldwide between 2011 and 2013.

Figure A.2. Price distribution of counterfeit electrical products of a given brand seized by customs authorities worldwide, 2011-2013

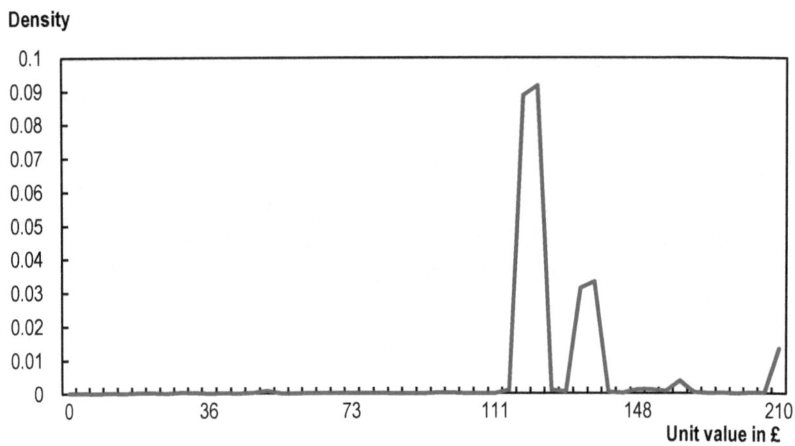

StatLink http://dx.doi.org/10.1787/888933553271

The identification of primary and secondary market using the methodology described in Step 2 implies that seized shipments of fake analysed electrical products associated with unit values strictly lower than GBP 129 are classified into the secondary market, whereas those associated with unit values larger than GBP 129 are classified into the primary market. This leads to the following results:

Table A.5. Share of the primary and secondary markets for counterfeit electrical products of the analysed brand seized by customs authorities worldwide, 2011-2013

	Freq.	Percent
Primary market	2,018	31.73
Secondary market	4,341	68.27
Total	**6,359**	**100**

In words, 32% of seized shipments of fake analysed electrical products between 2011 and 2013 were intended to be sold in the primary market and 68% in the secondary market.

Example 4

The clothing products of a given brand (HS 61) are the second most popular UK products seized worldwide. Figure A.3 below shows the price distribution of these products that were seized by customs authorities worldwide between 2011 and 2013.

Figure A.3. Price distribution of counterfeit clothes of the analysed brand seized by customs authorities worldwide, 2011-2013

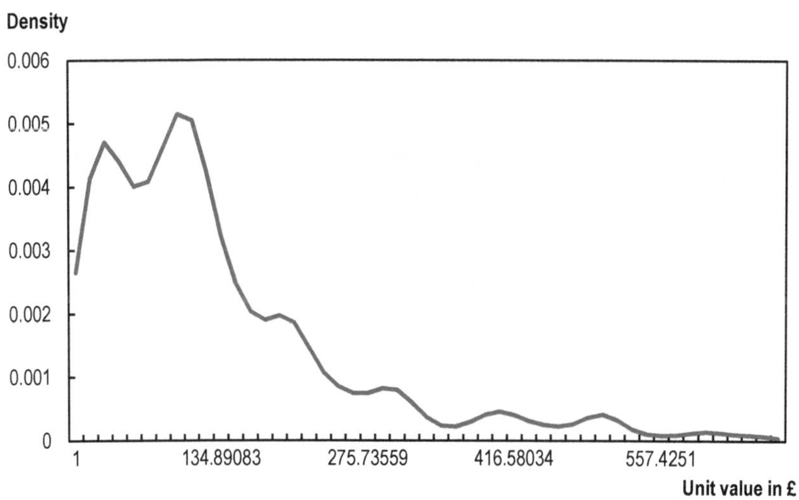

StatLink http://dx.doi.org/10.1787/888933553290

The identification of primary and secondary market using the methodology described previously implies that seized shipments of fake cloths of the analysed brand associated with unit values strictly lower than GBP 183 are classified into the secondary market, whereas those associated with unit values larger than GBP 183 are classified into the secondary market. This leads to the following results:

Table A.6. Share of the primary and secondary markets for counterfeit clothes of the analysed brand seized by customs authorities worldwide, 2011-2013

	Freq.	Percent
Primary market	776	39.19
Secondary market	1,204	60.81
Total	**1,980**	**100**

Thus, 39% of seized shipments of fake clothes of the analysed brand between 2011 and 2013 were intended to be sold in the primary market and 61% in the secondary market.

References

Hald, A. (1952), *Statistical Theory with Engineering Applications*, New York: John Wiley and Sons.

Verbeek, M. (2000), *A guide to modern econometrics*. Wilay, ISBN 0-470-85773-0.

Annex B. Tables

Table B.1. Propensity of economies to export counterfeit and pirated products to the UK

GTRIC-e for UK imports

Year	2011	2012	2013	Year	2011	2012	2013
Economy				Economy			
Afghanistan	0	0	0	Bosnia and Herzegovina	0	0	0
Albania	0	0	0	Botswana	0	0	0
Algeria	0	0	0	Bouvet Island	0	0	0
American Samoa	0	0	0	Brazil	0	0	0
Andorra	0	0	0	British Virgin Islands	0	0	0
Angola	0	0	0	Brunei Darussalam	0	0	0
Anguilla	0	0	0	Bulgaria	0	0	0
Antigua and Barbuda	0	0	0	Burkina Faso	0	0	0
Argentina	0	0	0	Burundi	0	0	0
Armenia	0	0	0	Cabo Verde	0	0	0
Aruba	0	0	0	Cambodia	0.137	0.053	0.065
Australia	0	0	0	Cameroon	0	0	0
Austria	0	0	0	Canada	0	0	0
Azerbaijan	0	0	0	Cayman Islands	0	0	0
Bahamas	0	0	0	Central African Republic	0	0	0
Bahrain	0	0	0	Chad	0	0	0
Bangladesh	0.471	0.284	0.318	Chile	0	0	0
Barbados	0	0	0	China (People's Republic of)	1.000	1.000	1.000

Table B.2. Propensity of economies to export counterfeit and pirated products to the UK

GTRIC-e for UK imports *(continued)*

Year	2011	2012	2013	Year	2011	2012	2013
Economy				Economy			
Belarus	0	0	0	Christmas Island	0	0	0
Belgium	0.247	0.116	0.136	Cocos (Keeling) Islands	0	0	0
Belize	0	0	0	Colombia	0	0	0
Benin	0	0	0	Comoros	0	0	0
Bolivia	0	0	0	Costa Rica	0	0	0
Cote d'Ivoire	0	0	0	Ghana	0.155	0.062	0.076
Croatia	0	0	0	Gibraltar	0	0	0
Cuba	0	0	0	Greece	0	0	0
Cote d'Ivoire	0	0	0	Ghana	0.155	0.062	0.076
Croatia	0	0	0	Gibraltar	0	0	0
Cuba	0	0	0	Greece	0	0	0
Curacao	0	0	0	Greenland	0	0	0
Cyprus[1]	0	0	0	Grenada	0	0	0
Czech Republic	0	0	0	Guam	0	0	0
Democratic People's Republic of Korea	0	0	0	Guatemala	0	0	0
Democratic Republic of Congo	0	0	0	Guinea	0	0	0
Denmark	0	0	0	Guinea-Bissau	0	0	
Djibouti	0	0	0	Guyana	0	0	0
Dominica	0	0	0	Haiti	0	0	0
Dominican Republic	0	0	0	Holy See	0	0	0

[1] Footnote by Turkey The information in this document with reference to « Cyprus » relates to the southern part of the Island. There is no single authority representing both Turkish and Greek Cypriot people on the Island. Turkey recognizes the Turkish Republic of Northern Cyprus (TRNC). Until a lasting and equitable solution is found within the context of the United Nations, Turkey shall preserve its position concerning the "Cyprus issue".2. Footnote by all the European Union Member States of the OECD and the European Union The Republic of Cyprus is recognised by all members of the United Nations with the exception of Turkey. The information in this document relates to the area under the effective control of the Government of the Republic of Cyprus.

Table B.1. Propensity of economies to export counterfeit and pirated products to the UK *(continued)*

Year Economy	2011	2012	2013	Year Economy	2011	2012	2013
Ecuador	0	0	0	Honduras	0	0	0
Egypt	0.255	0.121	0.142	Hong Kong (China)	1.000	1.000	1.000
El Salvador	0	0	0	Hungary	0.098	0.034	0.043
Equatorial Guinea	0	0	0	Iceland	0	0	0
Eritrea	0	0	0	India	0.752	0.571	0.609
Estonia	0	0	0	Indonesia	0.367	0.199	0.228
Ethiopia	0	0	0	Iran	0	0	0
Falkland Islands	0	0	0	Iraq	0	0	0
Faroe Islands	0	0	0	Ireland	0	0	0
Fiji	0	0	0	Israel	0	0	0
Finland	0	0	0	Italy	0.272	0.132	0.155
Former Yugoslav Republic of Macedonia	0	0	0	Jamaica	0	0	0
France	0	0	0	Japan	0	0	0
French Polynesia	0	0	0	Jordan	0	0	0
French Southern and Antartic Lands		0		Kazakhstan	0	0	0
Gabon	0	0	0	Kenya	0	0	0
Gambia	0	0	0	Kiribati	0	0	0
Georgia	0	0	0	Korea	0	0	0
Germany	0.076	0.025	0.031	Kuwait	0	0	0
Kyrgyzstan	0	0	0	Netherlands	0	0	0
Lao People's Democratic Republic	0	0	0	New Caledonia	0	0	0
Latvia	0.145	0.057	0.07	New Zealand	0	0	0
Lebanon	0	0	0	Nicaragua	0	0	0
Lesotho	0	0	0	Niger	0	0	0
Liberia	0	0	0	Nigeria	0.163	0.066	0.081

Table B.1. Propensity of economies to export counterfeit and pirated products to the UK (*continued*)

Year	2011	2012	2013	Year	2011	2012	2013
Economy				Economy			
Libya	0	0	0	Norway	0	0	0
Lithuania	0	0	0	Oman	0	0	0
Luxembourg	0	0	0	Pakistan	0.949	0.866	0.887
Macau (China)	0	0	0	Palestinian Authority*	0	0	0
Madagascar	0	0	0	Panama	0	0	0
Malawi	0	0	0	Papua New Guinea	0	0	0
Malaysia	0.435	0.254	0.286	Paraguay	0	0	0
Maldives	0	0	0	Peru	0	0	0
Mali	0	0	0	Philippines	0	0	0
Malta	0	0	0	Poland	0.248	0.116	0.137
Marshall Islands	0	0	0	Portugal	0	0	0
Mauritania	0	0	0	Qatar	0	0	0
Mauritius	0	0	0	Romania	0.113	0.041	0.051
Mexico	0	0	0	Russia	0	0	0
Micronesia	0	0	0	Rwanda	0	0	0
Moldova	0	0	0	Saint Helena	0	0	0
Mongolia	0	0	0	Saint Kitts and Nevis	0	0	0
Montenegro	0	0	0	Saint Lucia	0	0	0
Montserrat	0	0	0	Saint Vincent and the Grenadines	0	0	0
Morocco	0.221	0.099	0.118	Samoa	0	0	0
Mozambique	0	0	0	San Marino	0	0	0
Myanmar	0	0	0	Sao Tome and Principe	0	0	0
Namibia	0	0	0	Saudi Arabia	0	0	0
Nepal	0	0	0	Senegal	0	0	0
Niue		0		Seychelles	0	0	0
Norfolk Island	0	0	0	Sierra Leone	0	0	0

Table B.1. Propensity of economies to export counterfeit and pirated products to the UK (*end*)

Year	2011	2012	2013	Year	2011	2012	2013
Economy				Economy			
Singapore	0.333	0.175	0.201	Tonga	0	0	0
Slovak Republic	0	0	0	Trinidad and Tobago	0	0	0
Slovenia	0	0	0	Tunisia	0	0	0
Solomon Islands	0	0	0	Turkey	0.352	0.195	0.224
Somalia	0	0	0	Turkmenistan	0	0	0
South Africa	0	0	0	Turks and Caicos Islands	0	0	0
South Georgia and the South Sandwich Islands	0	0		Uganda	0	0	0
Spain	0	0	0	Ukraine	0	0	0
Sri Lanka	0.224	0.101	0.121	United Arab Emirates	0.415	0.237	0.269
Sudan	0	0	0	United Kingdom	0	0	0
Suriname	0	0	0	United States	0.247	0.116	0.136
Swaziland	0	0	0	United States Minor Outlying Islands	0	0	0
Sweden	0	0	0	Uruguay	0	0	0
Switzerland	0.076	0.024	0.031	Uzbekistan	0	0	0
Syrian Arab Republic	0.703	0.514	0.552	Vanuatu	0	0	0
Tajikistan	0	0	0	Venezuela	0	0	0
Tanzania	0	0	0	Viet Nam	0.237	0.109	0.130
Thailand	0.318	0.164	0.19	Yemen	0	0	0
Timor-Leste	0	0	0	Zambia	0	0	0
Togo	0	0	0	Zimbabwe	0	0	0

Table 0A.2. Propensity of product categories to suffer from counterfeiting in UK imports

GTRIC-p for UK imports

Year	2011	2012	2013
HS category			
Foodstuff (02-21)	0.110	0.114	0.110
Beverages (22)	0	0	0
Residues from the food industries (23)	0	0	0
Tobacco (24)	0	0	0
Salt; sulphur; earths and stone; lime and cement (25)	0	0	0
Ores, slag and ash (26)	0	0	0
Mineral fuels (27)	0	0	0
Organic and inorganic chemicals (28/29)	0	0	0
Pharmaceutical products (30)	0.471	0.479	0.472
Fertilisers (31)	0	0	0
Tanning or dyeing extracts (32)	0.165	0.171	0.166
Perfumery and cosmetics (33)	0.999	0.999	0.999
Soap; albuminoidal substances; glues; explosives (34-37)	0.032	0.034	0.032
Miscellaneous chemical products (38)	0	0	0
Plastic and articles thereof (39)	0.678	0.686	0.679
Rubber and article thereof (40)	0	0	0
Raw hides, skins and leather (41)	0	0	0
Articles of leather; handbags (42)	1.000	1.000	1.000
Furskins and artificial fur (43)	0	0	0
Wood and articles thereof (44)	0	0	0
Cork; straw and articles thereof (45/46)	0	0	0
Pulp and paper (47/48)	0.07	0.073	0.07
Printed articles (49)	0.126	0.131	0.127
Silk; wool; and other vegetable textile fibres (50-53)	0	0	0
Man-made filaments and staple fibres (54/55)	0	0	0
Wadding; cordage; ropes and articles thereof (56)	0	0	0
Carpets and rugs (57)	0	0	0

Table 0.2. Propensity of product categories to suffer from counterfeiting in UK imports *(end)*

Year	2011	2012	2013
HS category			
Finishing of textiles (58)	0.092	0.096	0.092
Other textiles n.e.c. (59)	0	0	0
Clothing, knitted or crocheted (61)	0.993	0.994	0.993
Clothing and accessories, not knitted or crocheted (62/65)	0.364	0.371	0.365
Other made-up textile articles (63)	0.333	0.341	0.334
Footwear (64)	1.000	1.000	1.000
Articles of stone, plaster and cement (68)	0	0	0
Ceramic products (69)	0.032	0.034	0.032
Glass and glassware (70)	0.075	0.078	0.075
Jewellery (71)	0.326	0.333	0.327
Iron and steel; and articles thereof (72/73)	0	0	0
Copper; nickel; aluminium; lead; zinc; tin; and articles thereof (74-81)	0	0	0
Tools and cutlery of base metal (82)	0.655	0.662	0.655
Miscellaneous articles of base metal (83)	0.129	0.134	0.13
Machinery and mechanical appliances (84)	0.159	0.164	0.16
Electrical machinery and electronics (85)	0.705	0.712	0.706
Railway (86)	0	0	0
Vehicles (87)	0.108	0.112	0.108
Aircraft (88)	0	0	0
Ships (89)	0	0	0
Optical; photographic; medical apparatus (90)	0.977	0.978	0.977
Watches (91)	1.000	1.000	1.000
Musical instruments (92)	0	0	0
Arms and ammunition (93)	0	0	0
Furnitures (94)	0.103	0.108	0.104
Toys and games (95)	0.758	0.764	0.758
Miscellaneous manufactured articles (66/67/96)	0.945	0.947	0.945

Table 0.3. Estimates of counterfeit and pirated imports to the UK, 2011-2013

Year	2011		2012		2013	
HS category \ Unit	Value in GBP mn	Share of imports	Value in GBP mn	Share of imports	Value in GBP mn	Share of imports
Foodstuff (02-21)	20.9	0.20%	23.9	0.20%	32.7	0.31%
Beverages (22)	0	0.00%	0	0.00%	0	0.00%
Residues from the food industries (23)	0	0.00%	0	0.00%	0	0.00%
Tobacco (24)	0	0.00%	0	0.00%	0	0.00%
Salt; sulphur; earths and stone; lime and cement (25)	0	0.00%	0	0.00%	0	0.00%
Ores, slag and ash (26)	0	0.00%	0	0.00%	0	0.00%
Mineral fuels (27)	0	0.00%	0	0.00%	0	0.00%
Organic and inorganic chemicals (28/29)	0	0.00%	0	0.00%	0	0.00%
Pharmaceutical products (30)	131	0.74%	145	0.79%	260	1.54%
Fertilisers (31)	0	0.00%	0	0.00%	0	0.00%
Tanning or dyeing extracts (32)	8.29	0.51%	8.62	0.49%	12.5	0.75%
Perfumery and cosmetics (33)	108	2.90%	126	3.08%	157	4.20%
Soap; albuminoidal substances; glues; explosives (34-37)	2.19	0.08%	2.4	0.09%	3.12	0.12%
Miscellaneous chemical products (38)	0	0.00%	0	0.00%	0	0.00%
Plastic and articles thereof (39)	306	2.71%	344	2.77%	428	3.47%
Rubber and article thereof (40)	0	0.00%	0	0.00%	0	0.00%
Raw hides, skins and leather (41)	0	0.00%	0	0.00%	0	0.00%
Articles of leather; handbags (42)	323	15.36%	329	14.46%	360	16.71%
Furskins and artificial fur (43)	0	0.00%	0	0.00%	0	0.00%
Wood and articles thereof (44)	0	0.00%	0	0.00%	0	0.00%
Cork; straw and articles thereof (45/46)	0	0.00%	0	0.00%	0	0.00%
Pulp and paper (47/48)	12	0.19%	12.9	0.20%	16.9	0.23%
Printed articles (49)	20.3	1.12%	19.7	1.13%	23.6	1.28%
Silk; wool; and other vegetable textile fibres (50-53)	0	0.00%	0	0.00%	0	0.00%
Man-made filaments and staple fibres (54/55)	0	0.00%	0	0.00%	0	0.00%

Table B.3. Estimates of counterfeit and pirated imports to the UK, 2011-2013 (*continued*)

Year	2011		2012		2013	
HS category / Unit	Value in GBP mn	Share of imports	Value in GBP mn	Share of imports	Value in GBP mn	Share of imports
Finishing of textiles (58)	1.61	0.81%	1.88	0.82%	2.21	0.99%
Other textiles n.e.c. (59)	0	0.00%	0	0.00%	0	0.00%
Knitted or crocheted fabrics (60)	0.53	0.33%	0.71	0.36%	0.52	0.33%
Clothing, knitted or crocheted (61)	908	11.60%	1030	12.06%	1300	14.48%
Clothing and accessories, not knitted or crocheted (62/65)	367	4.59%	383	4.55%	532	5.61%
Other made-up articles (63)	83.3	5.86%	87.6	5.69%	104	6.42%
Footwear (64)	484	12.15%	516	12.07%	585	13.86%
Articles of stone, plaster and cement (68)	0	0.00%	0	0.00%	0	0.00%
Ceramic products (69)	3.17	0.33%	2.82	0.26%	3.72	0.31%
Glass and glassware (70)	7.73	0.54%	8.33	0.54%	9.09	0.58%
Jewellery (71)	279	0.52%	141	0.59%	469	1.02%
Iron and steel; and articles thereof (72/72)	0	0.00%	0	0.00%	0	0.00%
Copper; nickel; aluminium; lead; zinc; tin; and articles thereof (74-81)	0	0.00%	0	0.00%	0	0.00%
Tools and cutlery of base metal (82)	71.4	5.94%	74.8	5.91%	83.7	6.91%
Miscellaneous articles of base metal (83)	18.4	1.22%	18.7	1.20%	20.5	1.27%
Machinery and mechanical appliances (84)	403	0.82%	429	0.82%	552	1.07%
Electrical machinery and electronics (85)	1740	4.87%	1910	5.02%	2480	6.19%
Railway (86)	0	0.00%	0	0.00%	0	0.00%
Vehicles (87)	72.5	0.19%	90.3	0.21%	147	0.33%
Aircraft (88)	0	0.00%	0	0.00%	0	0.00%
Ships (89)	0	0.00%	0	0.00%	0	0.00%

Table B.3. Estimates of counterfeit and pirated imports to the UK, 2011-2013 (*end*)

Year	2011		2012		2013	
HS category / Unit	Value in GBP mn	Share of imports	Value in GBP mn	Share of imports	Value in GBP mn	Share of imports
Optical; photographic; medical apparatus (90)	352	3.29%	403	3.44%	491	4.60%
Watches (91)	65.8	6.53%	74.5	6.53%	79.3	7.94%
Musical instruments (92)	0	0.00%	0	0.00%	0	0.00%
Toys and games (95)	506	14.49%	516	14.08%	661	14.73%
Miscellaneous manufactured articles (66/67/96)	137	9.61%	148	8.93%	137	13.97%
Total	**8521**	**2.96%**	**8938**	**3.20%**	**11049**	**4.04%**

Table 0.4. Propensity of economies to import fake goods infringing UK right holders' IP rights

UK GTRIC-e

Year	2011	2012	2013	Year	2011	2012	2013
Economy				Economy			
Afghanistan	0	0	0	Bolivia	0	0	0
Albania	0.282	0.381	0.402	Bonaire			0
Algeria	0.605	0.706	0.724	Bosnia and Herzegovina	0.499	0.607	0.628
American Samoa	0	0	0	Botswana	0	0	0
Andorra	0	0	0	Bouvet Island	0	0	0
Angola	0.53	0.636	0.656	Brazil	0	0	0
Anguilla	0	0	0	British Indian Ocean Territory	0		0
Antarctica	0	0	0	British Virgin Islands	0	0	0
Antigua and Barbuda	0	0	0	Brunei Darussalam	0	0	0
Argentina	0	0	0	Bulgaria	0.937	0.964	0.968
Aruba	0	0	0	Burundi	0	0	0
Australia	0.426	0.534	0.556	Côte d'Ivoire	0	0	0
Austria	0.429	0.538	0.559	Cabo Verde	0	0	0
Azerbaijan	0	0	0	Cambodia	0	0	0
Bahamas	0.097	0.153	0.166	Cameroon	0	0	0
Bahrain	0	0	0	Canada	0.098	0.154	0.168

Table B.4. Propensity of economies to import fake goods infringing UK right holders' IP rights (*continued*)

Year	2011	2012	2013	Year	2011	2012	2013
Economy				Economy			
Bangladesh	0	0	0	Cayman Islands	0	0	0
Barbados	0	0	0	Central African Republic	0	0	0
Belarus	0	0	0	Chad	0	0	0
Belgium	0.480	0.588	0.609	Chile	0.115	0.176	0.191
Belize	0	0	0	China (People's Republic of)	0.098	0.154	0.167
Benin	0	0	0	Christmas Island	0		
Bermuda	0	0	0	Cocos (Keeling) Islands	0	0	0
Bhutan	0	0	0	Colombia	0.219	0.307	0.327
Comoros	0.731	0.813	0.828	Gambia	0	0	0
Congo	0	0	0	Georgia	0	0	0
Cook Islands	0	0	0	Germany	0.432	0.541	0.562
Costa Rica	0	0	0	Ghana	0.297	0.398	0.419
Croatia	0.248	0.342	0.362	Gibraltar	0	0	0
Cuba	0	0	0	Greece	0	0	0
Curaçao	0	0	0	Greenland	0	0	0
Cyprus[2]	0.596	0.697	0.716	Grenada	0	0	0
Czech Republic	0.956	0.976	0.979	Guam	0	0	0
Democratic People's Republic of Korea	0	0	0	Guatemala	0	0	0

[2] Footnote by Turkey The information in this document with reference to « Cyprus » relates to the southern part of the Island. There is no single authority representing both Turkish and Greek Cypriot people on the Island. Turkey recognizes the Turkish Republic of Northern Cyprus (TRNC). Until a lasting and equitable solution is found within the context of the United Nations, Turkey shall preserve its position concerning the "Cyprus issue".2. Footnote by all the European Union Member States of the OECD and the European Union The Republic of Cyprus is recognised by all members of the United Nations with the exception of Turkey. The information in this document relates to the area under the effective control of the Government of the Republic of Cyprus.

Table B.4. Propensity of economies to import fake goods infringing UK right holders' IP rights (*continued*)

Year	2011	2012	2013	Year	2011	2012	2013
Economy				Economy			
Democratic Republic of the Congo	0.841	0.898	0.908	Guinea	0.299	0.399	0.42
Denmark	0.352	0.458	0.479	Guinea-Bissau	0	0	0
Djibouti	0	0	0	Guyana	0	0	0
Dominican Republic	0	0	0	Heard Island and Mcdonald Islands	0		0
Ecuador	0	0	0	Holy See	0	0	0
Egypt	0	0	0	Honduras	0	0	0
El Salvador	0	0	0	Hong Kong (China)	0.214	0.301	0.321
Equatorial Guinea	0	0	0	Hungary	0.605	0.705	0.724
Eritrea	0	0	0	Iceland	0	0	0
Estonia	0.647	0.742	0.76	India	0	0	0
Ethiopia	0	0	0	Indonesia	0	0	0
Falkland Islands (Malvinas)	0	0	0	Iran	0	0	0
Faroe Islands	0	0	0	Iraq	0	0	0
Fiji	0	0	0	Ireland	0.335	0.439	0.46
Finland	0.583	0.685	0.704	Israel	0	0	0
Former Yugoslav Republic of Macedonia	0.372	0.478	0.5	Italy	0.645	0.74	0.758
France	0.454	0.563	0.584	Jamaica	0	0	0
French Polynesia	0	0	0	Japan	0.242	0.335	0.355
French Southern and Antartic Lands	0	0	0	Jordan	0.739	0.819	0.833
Gabon	0.096	0.151	0.164	Kazakhstan	0	0	0
Kenya	0.558	0.663	0.682	Mozambique	0	0	0
Kiribati	0	0	0	Myanmar	0	0	0
Korea	0.118	0.181	0.196	Namibia	0.308	0.409	0.431
Kuwait	0.527	0.633	0.654	Nauru	0	0	0
Kyrgyzstan	0	0	0	Nepal	0	0	0

Table B.4. Propensity of economies to import fake goods infringing UK right holders' IP rights (*continued*)

Year	2011	2012	2013	Year	2011	2012	2013
Economy				Economy			
Lao People's Democratic Republic	0	0	0	Netherlands	0.502	0.609	0.63
Latvia	0.671	0.763	0.78	New Caledonia	0	0	0
Lebanon	0	0	0	New Zealand	0.146	0.217	0.234
Lesotho	0	0	0	Nicaragua	0	0	0
Liberia	0	0	0	Niger	0	0	0
Libya	0.259	0.355	0.375	Nigeria	0	0	0
Lithuania	0.454	0.563	0.584	Niue	0	0	0
Luxembourg	0.408	0.516	0.538	Norfolk Island	0	0	0
Macau (China)	0	0	0	Northern Mariana Islands	0	0	0
Madagascar	0	0	0	Norway	0.346	0.45	0.472
Malawi	0	0	0	Oman	0	0	0
Malaysia	0	0	0	Pakistan	0	0	0
Maldives	0	0	0	Palau	0	0	0
Mali	0.487	0.595	0.616	Palestinian Authority*	0	0	0
Malta	0.95	0.972	0.976	Panama	0	0	0
Marshall Islands	0	0	0	Papua New Guinea	0	0	0
Mauritania	0	0	0	Paraguay	0	0	0
Mauritius	0.507	0.614	0.635	Peru	0	0	0
Mayotte	0	0	0	Philippines	0	0	0
Mexico	0.258	0.353	0.374	Pitcairn	0	0	0
Micronesia	0	0	0	Poland	0.312	0.414	0.436
Moldova	0	0	0	Portugal	0.768	0.842	0.855
Mongolia	0	0	0	Qatar	0	0	0
Montenegro	0.402	0.510	0.532	Romania	0.76	0.836	0.849
Montserrat	0	0	0	Russia	0.401	0.509	0.531
Morocco	0.715	0.800	0.815	Rwanda	0	0	0
Saint Helena	0	0	0	Tanzania	0.59	0.692	0.711
Saint Kitts and Nevis	0	0	0	Thailand	0	0	0
Saint Lucia	0	0	0	Timor-Leste	0	0	0

Table B.4. Propensity of economies to import fake goods infringing UK right holders' IP rights (*continued*)

Year	2011	2012	2013	Year	2011	2012	2013
Economy				Economy			
Saint Pierre and Miquelon	0	0	0	Swaziland	0	0	0
Saint Vincent and the Grenadines	0	0	0	Sweden	0.344	0.449	0.47
Samoa	0	0	0	Switzerland	0.213	0.3	0.319
San Marino	0.808	0.874	0.885	Togo	0.654	0.749	0.766
Sao Tome and Principe	0	0	0	Syrian Arab Republic	0	0	0
Saudi Arabia	0.393	0.501	0.523	Tajikistan	0	0	0
Senegal	0.1	0.157	0.17	Tonga	0	0	0
Serbia	0.393	0.501	0.523	Trinidad and Tobago	0	0	0
Seychelles	0	0	0	Tunisia	0	0	0
Sierra Leone	0	0	0	Turkey	0.099	0.155	0.168
Singapore	0	0	0	Turkmenistan	0	0	0
Sint Maarten			0	Turks and Caicos Islands	0	0	0
Slovak Republic	0.514	0.621	0.642	Uganda	0	0	0
Slovenia	0.855	0.909	0.917	Ukraine	0.359	0.465	0.487
Solomon Islands	0	0	0	United Arab Emirates	0	0	0
Somalia	0.13	0.197	0.212	United Kingdom	0.359	0.465	0.487
South Africa	0	0	0	United States	0.323	0.426	0.447
South Georgia and the South Sandwich Islands	0	0		United States Minor Outlying Islands	0		0
South Sudan			0	Uruguay	0	0	0
Spain	0.515	0.622	0.643	Uzbekistan	0	0	0
Sri Lanka	0	0	0	Vanuatu	0	0	0
Sudan	0	0	0	Venezuela	0.243	0.335	0.355
Suriname	0	0	0	Viet Nam	0	0	0

Table B.4. Propensity of economies to import fake goods infringing UK right holders' IP rights (*end*)

Year	2011	2012	2013	Year	2011	2012	2013
Economy				Economy			
Wallis and Futuna	0	0	0	Zambia	0	0	0
Western Sahara			0	Zimbabwe	0	0	0
Yemen	0.293	0.393	0.414				

Table 0.5. Propensity for product categories to suffer from infringements of UK IPRs

Year	2011	2012	2013	Year	2011	2012	2013
HS category				HS category			
Foodstuff (02-21)	0.215	0.435	0.428	Other textiles n.e.c. (59)	0	0	0
Beverages (22)	0.053	0.162	0.159	Knitted or crocheted fabrics (60)	0.906	0.975	0.974
Residues from the food industries (23)	0	0	0	Clothing, knitted or crocheted (61)	1.000	1.000	1.000
Tobacco (24)	1.000	1.000	1.000	Clothing and accessories, not knitted or crocheted (62/65)	1.000	1.000	1.000
Salt; sulphur; earths and stone; lime (25)	0	0	0	Other made-up textile articles (63)	0.17	0.371	0.365
Ores, slag and ash (26)	0	0	0	Footwear (64)	1.000	1.000	1.000
Mineral fuels (27)	0.021	0.082	0.079	Articles of stone, plaster and cement (68)	0	0	0
Organic and inorganic chemicals (28/29)	0	0	0	Ceramic products (69)	0.021	0.081	0.079
Pharmaceutical products (30)	0.576	0.792	0.788	Glass and glassware (70)	0.055	0.168	0.164
Fertilisers (31)	0	0	0	Jewellery (71)	0.126	0.302	0.297
Tanning or dyeing extracts (32)	0	0	0	Iron and steel (72/73)	0.023	0.088	0.085
Perfumery and cosmetics (33)	0.852	0.954	0.952	Copper; nickel; aluminium; lead (74-81)	0	0	0
Soap; albuminoidal substances; glues (34-37)	0.022	0.084	0.081	Tools and cutlery of base metal (82)	0.157	0.351	0.345
Miscellaneous chemical products (38)	0.162	0.359	0.353	Miscellaneous base metal articles (83)	0.064	0.187	0.183
Plastic and articles thereof (39)	0.381	0.625	0.619	Machinery and mechanical appliances (84)	0.052	0.161	0.157

Table 0.5. Propensity for product categories to suffer from infringements of UK IPRs *(end)*

Year	2011	2012	2013	Year	2011	2012	2013
HS category				HS category			
Rubber and article thereof (40)	0.123	0.297	0.291	Electrical machinery and electronics (85)	0.178	0.382	0.376
Raw hides, skins and leather (41)	0	0	0	Railway (86)	0	0	0
Articles of leather; handbags (42)	1.000	1.000	1.000	Vehicles (87)	0.106	0.267	0.262
Furskins and artificial fur (43)	0	0	0	Aircraft (88)	0	0	0
Wood and articles thereof (44)	0	0	0	Ships (89)	0	0	0
Cork; straw and articles thereof (45/46)	0	0	0	Optical; photo.; medical apparatus (90)	0.122	0.295	0.29
Pulp and paper (47/48)	0.138	0.322	0.317	Watches (91)	0.777	0.918	0.916
Printed articles (49)	0.103	0.263	0.258	Musical instruments (92)	0.024	0.09	0.087
Silk; wool; and other vegetable textile fibres (50-53)	0	0	0	Arms and ammunition (93)	0	0	0
Man-made filaments and staple fibres (54/55)	0	0	0	Furniture (94)	0.023	0.088	0.086
Wadding; cordage; ropes (56)	0	0	0	Toys and games (95)	0.998	1.000	1.000
Carpets and rugs (57)	0	0	0	Miscellaneous (66/67/96)	0.58	0.796	0.791
Finishing of textiles (58)	0.132	0.312	0.307				

Table 0.6. Correspondences between sectors, HS product categories and NACE industries

Sector	HS code	HS category	NACE code	NACE category
Food, beverages and tobacco	15/21	Foodstuff	1011	Processing and preserving of meat
			1012	Processing and preserving of poultry meat
			1013	Production of meat and poultry meat
			1020	Processing and preserving of fish, crustaceans and molluscs
			1031	Processing and preserving of potatoes
			1032	Manufacture of fruit and vegetable juice
			1039	Other processing and preserving of fruit
			1041	Manufacture of oils and fats
			1042	Manufacture of margarine and similar fats
			1051	Operation of dairies and cheese making
			1052	Manufacture of ice cream
			1071	Manufacture of bread; manufacture of fresh pastry goods and cakes
			1072	Manufacture of rusks and biscuits; manufacture of preserved pastry goods
			1081	Manufacture of sugar
			1082	Manufacture of cocoa, chocolate and sugar
			1073	Manufacture of macaroni, noodles, couscous and similar farinaceous products
			1085	Manufacture of prepared meals and dishes
			1084	Manufacture of condiments and seasonings
			1086	Manufacture of homogenised food preparations and dietetic food
			1089	Manufacture of other food products n.e.c.

Table 0.6. Correspondences between sectors, HS product categories and NACE industries *(continued)*

Sector	HS code	HS category	NACE code	NACE category
Food, beverages and tobacco	22	Beverages, spirits and vinegar.	1100	Manufacture of beverages
Food, beverages and tobacco	23	Residues from the food industries; animal fodder.	1091	Manufacture of prepared feeds for farm animals
			1092	Manufacture of prepared pet foods
Food, beverages and tobacco	24	Tobacco and manufactured tobacco substitutes.	1200	Manufacture of tobacco products
Mineral products (e.g. fuels, ores)	25	Salt; sulphur; earths and stone; lime and cement.	0811	Quarrying of ornamental and building stone, limestone, gypsum, chalk and slate
			0812	Operation of gravel and sand pits; mining of clays and kaolin
			0890	Mining and quarrying n.e.c.
Mineral products (e.g. fuels, ores)	26	Ores, slag and ash.	0710	Mining of iron ores
			0720	Mining of non-ferrous metal ores
Chemical and allied products	28 - 29	Organic and inorganic chemicals, rare-earth metals, radioactive elements or isotopes.	2011	Manufacture of industrial gases
			2012	Manufacture of dyes and pigments
			2013	Manufacture of other inorganic basic chemical
			2014	Manufacture of other organic basic chemicals
Pharmaceutical and medicinal chemical products	30	Pharmaceutical products.	2110	Manufacture of basic pharmaceuticals
			2120	Manufacture of pharmaceutical preparations
Chemical and allied products	31	Fertilisers.	2015	Manufacture of fertilisers and nitrogen compounds
Chemical and allied products	32	Tanning or dyeing extracts; dyes, pigments; paints and varnishes; putty and inks.	2030	Manufacture of paints, varnishes and similar coatings, printing ink and mastics
Perfumery and cosmetics	33	Essential oils and resinoids; perfumery, cosmetic or toilet preparations.	2042	Manufacture of perfumes
			2053	Manufacture of essential oils

Table 0.6. Correspondences between sectors, HS product categories and NACE industries *(continued)*

Sector	HS code	HS category	NACE code	NACE category
Chemical and allied products	34 - 37	Soap, waxes, scouring products, candles; albuminoidal substances, starches; glues; enzymes; explosives, matches; pyrophoric products.	2041	Manufacture of soap and detergents, cleaning and polishing preparations
			2051	Manufacture of explosives
			2052	Manufacture of glues
			2059	Manufacture of other chemical products
Chemical and allied products	38	Miscellaneous chemical products.	2020	Manufacture of pesticides and other agrochemical products
Textiles and other intermediate products	39	Plastics and articles thereof.	2016	Manufacture of plastics in primary forms
			2221	Manufacture of plastic plates, sheets, tubes
			2222	Manufacture of plastic packing goods
			2223	Manufacture of builders' ware of plastic
			2229	Manufacture of other plastic products
Textiles and other intermediate products	40	Rubber and articles thereof.	2017	Manufacture of synthetic rubber
			2211	Manufacture of rubber tyres and tubes
			2219	Manufacture of other rubber products
Textiles and other intermediate products	41	Raw hides, skins and leather.	1411	Manufacture of leather clothes
			1511	Tanning and dressing of leather; of fur
Clothing, footwear, leather and related products	42	Articles of leather; saddlery and harness; travel goods, handbags; articles of gut.	1512	Manufacture of luggage, handbags and the like, saddlery and harness
Clothing, footwear, leather and related products	43	Furskins and artificial fur; manufactures thereof.	1420	Manufacture of articles of fur

Table B.6. Correspondences between sectors, HS product categories and NACE industries (*continued*)

Sector	HS code	HS category	NACE code	NACE category
Textiles and other intermediate products	44	Wood and articles of wood; wood charcoal.	1620	Sawmilling and planning of wood
			1621	Manufacture of products of wood, cork, straw and plaiting materials
			1622	Manufacture of veneer sheets
			1623	Manufacture of other builders' carpentry
Textiles and other intermediate products	45 - 46	Cork and articles of cork; Manufactures of straw or of other plaiting materials; basketware and wickerwork.	1629	Manufacture of other products of wood; manufacture of articles of cork, straw and plaiting materials
Textiles and other intermediate products	47 - 48	Pulp of wood or of other fibrous cellulosic material; recovered (waste and scrap) paper or paperboard; Paper and paperboard; articles of paper pulp, of paper or of paperboard.	1711	Manufacture of pulp
			1712	Manufacture of paper
			1721	Manufacture of corrugated paper and paperboard and of containers of paper
			1722	Manufacture of household and sanitary goods and of toilet requisites
			1723	Manufacture of paper stationery
			1724	Manufacture of wallpaper
			1729	Manufacture of other articles of paper
Household cultural and recreation goods	49	Printed books, newspapers, pictures; manuscripts, typescripts and plans.	1811	Printing of newspapers
			1812	Other printing
			1813	Pre-press and pre-media services
			1814	Binding and related services
			1820	Reproduction of recorded media

Table B.6. Correspondences between sectors, HS product categories and NACE industries (*continued*)

Sector	HS code	HS category	NACE code	NACE category
Textiles and other intermediate products	50 - 53	Silk; wool, fine or coarse animal hair; cotton; other vegetable textile fibres.	1310	Preparation and spinning of textile fibres
			1320	Weaving of textiles
Textiles and other intermediate products	54 - 55	Man-made filaments and staple fibres	2060	Manufacture of man-made fibres
Textiles and other intermediate products	56	Wadding, felt and nonwovens; special yarns; twine, cordage, ropes and cables and articles thereof.	1394	Manufacture of cordage, rope, twine
Textiles and other intermediate products	57	Carpets and other textile floor coverings.	1393	Manufacture of carpets and rugs
Textiles and other intermediate products	58	Special woven fabrics; tufted textile fabrics; lace; tapestries; trimmings; embroidery;	1330	Finishing of textiles
Textiles and other intermediate products	59	Impregnated, coated, covered or laminated textile fabrics; textile articles of a kind suitable for industrial use.	1395	Manufacture of non-wovens and articles made from non-wovens, except apparel
			1396	Manufacture of other technical textiles
			1399	Manufacture of other textiles n.e.c.
Clothing, footwear, leather and related products	60	Knitted or crocheted fabrics.	1391	Manufacture of knitted and crocheted fabrics
Clothing, footwear, leather and related products	61	Articles of apparel and clothing accessories, knitted or crocheted.	1431	Manufacture of knitted hosiery
			1439	Manufacture of other knitted and crocheted apparel
Clothing, footwear, leather and related products	62 - 65	Articles of apparel and clothing accessories, not knitted or crocheted;	1412	Manufacture of workwear
			1413	Manufacture of other outerwear
			1414	Manufacture of underwear
			1419	Manufacture of other wearing apparel
Clothing, footwear, leather and related products	63	Other made up textile articles; sets; worn clothing and worn textile articles; rags.	1392	Manufacture of made-up textiles
Clothing, footwear, leather and related products	64	Footwear, gaiters and the like; parts of such articles.	1520	Manufacture of footwear

Table B.6. Correspondences between sectors, HS product categories and NACE industries (*continued*)

Sector	HS code	HS category	NACE code	NACE category
Non-metallic mineral products (e.g. glass and glass products, ceramic products)	68	Articles of stone, plaster, cement, asbestos, mica or similar materials.	2351	Manufacture of cement
			2352	Manufacture of lime and plaster
Non-metallic mineral products (e.g. glass and glass products, ceramic products)	68	Articles of stone, plaster, cement, asbestos, mica or similar materials.	2361	Manufacture of concrete products for construction purposes
			2362	Manufacture of plaster products for construction purposes
			2363	Manufacture of ready-mixed concrete
			2364	Manufacture of mortars
			2365	Manufacture of fibre cement
			2369	Manufacture of other articles of concrete, plaster and cement
			2370	Cutting, shaping and finishing of stone
			2391	Production of abrasive products
			2399	Manufacture of other non-metallic mineral products n.e.c.
Clothing, footwear, leather and related products	61	Articles of apparel and clothing accessories, knitted or crocheted.	1431	Manufacture of knitted hosiery
			1439	Manufacture of other knitted and crocheted apparel

Table B.6. Correspondences between sectors, HS product categories and NACE industries (*continued*)

Sector	HS code	HS category	NACE code	NACE category
Non-metallic mineral products (e.g. glass and glass products, ceramic products)	69	Ceramic products.	2320	Manufacture of refractory products
			2331	Manufacture of ceramic tiles and flags
			2332	Manufacture of bricks, tiles and construction products, in baked clay
			2341	Manufacture of ceramic household and ornamental articles
			2342	Manufacture of ceramic sanitary fixtures
			2343	Manufacture of ceramic insulators and insulating fittings
			2344	Manufacture of other technical ceramic products
			2349	Manufacture of other ceramic products
			2311	Manufacture of flat lgass
Non-metallic mineral products (e.g. glass and glass products, ceramic products)	70	Glass and glassware.	2312	Shaping and processing of flat glass
			2313	Manufacture of hollow glass
			2314	Manufacture of glass fibres
			2312	Shaping and processing of flat glass
			2313	Manufacture of hollow glass
			2314	Manufacture of glass fibres
			3212	Manufacture of jewellery and related articles
			3213	Manufacture of imitation jewellery and related articles

Table B.6. Correspondences between sectors, HS product categories and NACE industries (*continued*)

Sector	HS code	HS category	NACE code	NACE category
Basic metals and fabricated metal products	72 - 73	Iron and steel; and articles thereof.	2410	Manufacture of basic iron and steel and of ferroalloys
			2420	Manufacture of tubes, pipes, hollow profiles and related fittings, of steel
			2431	Cold drawing of bars
			2432	Cold rolling of narrow strip
			2433	Cold forming or folding
			2434	Cold drawing of wire
			2451	Casting of iron
			2452	Casting of steel
			2521	Manufacture of central heating radiators and boilers
			2529	Manufacture of other tanks, reservoirs and containers of metal
Basic metals and fabricated metal products	74-81	Copper; nickel; aluminium; lead; zinc; tin; other base metals and articles thereof.	2454	Casting of other non-ferrous metals
			2511	Manufacture of metal structures and parts of structures
			2512	Manufacture of doors and windows of meta
Basic metals and fabricated metal products	82	Tools, implements, cutlery, spoons and forks, of base metal; parts thereof of base metal.	2571	Manufacture of cutlery
			2572	Manufacture of locks and hinges
			2573	Manufacture of tools
Basic metals and fabricated metal products	82	Tools, implements, cutlery, spoons and forks, of base metal; parts thereof of base metal.	2571	Manufacture of cutlery
			2572	Manufacture of locks and hinges
			2573	Manufacture of tools

Table B.6. Correspondences between sectors, HS product categories and NACE industries *(continued)*

Sector	HS code	HS category	NACE code	NACE category
Basic metals and fabricated metal products	83	Miscellaneous articles of base metal.	2591	Manufacture of steel drums
			2592	Manufacture of light metal packaging
			2593	Manufacture of wire products, chain and springs
			2594	Manufacture of fasteners and screw machine
			2599	Manufacture of other metal products
Machinery, industrial equipment; computers and peripheral equipment; ships and aircrafts	84	Nuclear reactors, boilers, machinery and mechanical appliances; parts thereof.	2530	Manufacture of steam generators, except central heating hot water boilers
			2550	Forging, pressing, stamping and roll-forming of metal; powder metallurgy
			2561	Treatment and coating of metals
			2562	Machining
			2810	Manufacture of general " purpose machinery
			2820	Manufacture of other general-purpose machinery
			2830	Manufacture of agricultural and forestry machinery
			2840	Manufacture of metal forming machinery and machine tools
			2890	Manufacture of other special-purpose machinery
			2620	Manufacture of computers and peripheral equipment

Table B.6. Correspondences between sectors, HS product categories and NACE industries (*continued*)

Sector	HS code	HS category	NACE code	NACE category
Electrical household appliances, electronic and telecommunications equipment	85	Electrical machinery and equipment and parts thereof; sound recorders and reproducers, television image and sound recorders and reproducers, and parts and accessories of such articles.	2611	Manufacture of electronic components
			2612	Manufacture of loaded electronic boards
			2630	Manufacture of communication equipment
			2640	Manufacture of consumer electronics
			2680	Manufacture of magnetic and optical media
			2711	Manufacture of electric motors, generators and transformers
			2712	Manufacture of electricity distribution and control apparatus
			2720	Manufacture of batteries and accumulators
			2731	Manufacture of fibre optic cables
			2732	Manufacture of other electronic and electric wires and cables
			2733	Manufacture of wiring devices
			2751	Manufacture of electric domestic appliances
			2752	Manufacture of non-electric domestic appliances
			2790	Manufacture of other electrical equipment

Table B.6. Correspondences between sectors, HS product categories and NACE industries (*continued*)

Machinery, industrial equipment; computers and peripheral equipment; ships and aircrafts	86	Railway or tramway locomotives, rolling-stock and parts thereof; railway or tramway track fixtures and fittings and parts thereof; mechanical (including electro-mechanical) traffic signalling equipment of all kinds.	3020	Manufacture of railway locomotives and rolling stock
Motor vehicles and motorcycles	87	Vehicles other than railway or tramway rolling-stock, and parts and accessories thereof.	2910	Manufacture of motor vehicles
			2920	Manufacture of bodies (coachwork) for motor vehicles; manufacture of trailers and semi-trailers
			2931	Manufacture of electrical and electronic equipment for motor vehicles
			2932	Manufacture of other parts and accessories for motor vehicles
			3091	Manufacture of motorcycles
			3092	Manufacture of bicycles and invalid carriages
			3099	Manufacture of other transport equipment n.e.c.
Machinery, industrial equipment; computers and peripheral equipment; ships and aircrafts	88	Aircraft, spacecraft, and parts thereof.	3030	Manufacture of air and spacecraft and related machinery

Table B.6. Correspondences between sectors, HS product categories and NACE industries (*continued*)

Sector	HS code	HS category	NACE code	NACE category
Machinery, industrial equipment; computers and peripheral equipment; ships and aircrafts	89	Ships, boats and floating structures.	3011	Building of ships and floating structures
			3012	Building of pleasure and sporting boats
Electrical household appliances, electronic and telecommunications equipment	90	Optical, photographic, cinematographic, measuring, checking, precision, medical or surgical instruments and apparatus; parts and accessories thereof.	2651	Manufacture of instruments and appliances for measuring, testing and navigation
			2660	Manufacture of irradiation, electro medical and electrotherapeutic equipment
			2670	Manufacture of optical instruments and photographic equipment
			3250	Manufacture of medical and dental instruments and supplies
Watches and jewellery	91	Clocks and watches and parts thereof.	2652	Manufacture of watches and clocks
Household cultural and recreation goods;	92	Musical instruments; parts and accessories of such articles.	3220	Manufacture of musical instruments
Machinery, industrial equipment; computers and peripheral equipment; ships and aircrafts	93	Arms and ammunition; parts and accessories thereof.	2540	Manufacture of weapons and ammunition
			3040	Manufacture of military fighting vehicles
Furniture, lighting equipment, carpets and other manufacturing n.e.c	94	Furniture; bedding, mattresses, mattress supports; lamps and lighting fittings; illuminated signs and the like; prefabricated buildings.	2740	Manufacture of electric lighting equipment
			3101	Manufacture of office and shop furniture
			3102	Manufacture of kitchen furniture
			3103	Manufacture of mattresses
			3109	Manufacture of other furniture

Table B.6. Correspondences between sectors, HS product categories and NACE industries (*end*)

Sector	HS code	HS category	NACE code	NACE category
Household cultural and recreation goods	95	Toys, games and sports requisites; parts and accessories thereof.	3230	Manufacture of sports goods
			3240	Manufacture of games and toys
Furniture, lighting equipment, carpets and other manufacturing n.e.c	96; 66; 67	Miscellaneous manufactured articles	3291	Manufactures of brooms and brushes
			3299	Other manufacturing n.e.c.

Table 0.7. Correspondences between sectors and NACE retail and wholesale industries

Sector	NACE code	NACE description
Food, beverages and tobacco	4617	Agents involved in the sale of food, beverages and tobacco
	4631	Wholesale of fruit and vegetables
	4632	Wholesale of meat and meat products
	4633	Wholesale of dairy products, eggs and edible oils and fats
	4634	Wholesale of beverages
	4635	Wholesale of tobacco products
	4636	Wholesale of sugar and chocolate and sugar confectionery
	4637	Wholesale of coffee, tea, cocoa and spices
	4638	Wholesale of other food, including fish, crustaceans and molluscs
	4639	Non-specialised wholesale of food, beverages and tobacco
	4711	Retail sale in non-specialised stores with food, beverages or tobacco predominating
	4721	Retail sale of fruit and vegetables in specialised stores
	4722	Retail sale of meat and meat products in specialised stores
	4723	Retail sale of fish, crustaceans and molluscs in specialised stores
	4724	Retail sale of bread, cakes, flour confectionery and sugar confectionery in specialised stores
	4725	Retail sale of beverages in specialised stores
	4726	Retail sale of tobacco products in specialised stores
	4729	Other retail sale of food in specialised stores
	4781	Retail sale via stalls and markets of food, beverages and tobacco products
Mineral products (e.g. fuels, ores)	4730	Retail sale of automotive fuel in specialised stores
	4612	Agents involved in the sale of fuels, ores, metals and industrial chemicals
	4671	Wholesale of solid, liquid and gaseous fuels and related products

Table 0.7. Correspondences between sectors and NACE retail and wholesale industries *(continued)*

Chemical and allied products	4675	Wholesale of chemical products
Pharmaceutical and medicinal chemical products	4646	Wholesale of pharmaceutical goods
Perfumery and cosmetics	4645	Wholesale of perfume and cosmetics
	4775	Retail sale of cosmetic and toilet articles in specialised stores
Textiles and other intermediate products	4641	Wholesale of textiles
	4673	Wholesale of wood, construction materials and sanitary equipment
	4676	Wholesale of other intermediate products
	4751	Retail sale of textiles in specialised stores
Clothing, footwear, leather and related products	4616	Agents involved in the sale of textiles, clothing, fur, footwear and leather goods
	4642	Wholesale of clothing and footwear
	4771	Retail sale of clothing in specialised stores
	4772	Retail sale of footwear and leather goods in specialised stores
	4773	Dispensing chemist in specialised stores
	4782	Retail sale via stalls and markets of textiles, clothing and footwear
Watches and jewellery	4648	Wholesale of watches and jewellery
	4777	Retail sale of watches and jewellery in specialised stores
Non-metallic mineral products	4644	Wholesale of china and glassware and cleaning materials
	4752	Retail sale of hardware, paints and glass in specialised stores
Basic metals and fabricated metal products	4613	Agents involved in the sale of timber and building materials
	4672	Wholesale of metals and metal ores
	4674	Wholesale of hardware, plumbing and heating equipment and supplies
	4677	Wholesale of waste and scrap

Table 0.7. Correspondences between sectors and NACE retail and wholesale industries *(continued)*

Sector	NACE code	NACE category
Electrical household appliances, electronic and telecommunications equipment	4643	Wholesale of electrical household appliances
	4652	Wholesale of electronic and telecommunications equipment and parts
	4742	Retail sale of telecommunications equipment in specialised stores
	4743	Retail sale of audio and video equipment in specialised stores
	4754	Retail sale of electrical household appliances in specialised stores
	4774	Retail sale of medical and orthopaedic goods in specialised stores
Electrical household appliances, electronic and telecommunications equipment	4643	Wholesale of electrical household appliances
	4652	Wholesale of electronic and telecommunications equipment and parts
	4742	Retail sale of telecommunications equipment in specialised stores
	4743	Retail sale of audio and video equipment in specialised stores
	4754	Retail sale of electrical household appliances in specialised stores
	4774	Retail sale of medical and orthopaedic goods in specialised stores
Machinery, industrial equipment; computers and peripheral equipment; ships and aircrafts	4614	Agents involved in the sale of machinery, industrial equipment, ships and aircraft
	4651	Wholesale of computers, computer peripheral equipment and software
	4661	Wholesale of agricultural machinery, equipment and supplies
	4662	Wholesale of machine tools
	4663	Wholesale of mining, construction and civil engineering machinery
	4664	Wholesale of machinery for the textile industry and of sewing and knitting machines
	4666	Wholesale of other office machinery and equipment
	4669	Wholesale of other machinery and equipment
	4741	Retail sale of computers, peripheral units and software in specialised stores

Table B.7. Correspondences between sectors and NACE retail and wholesale industries (*end*)

Sector	NACE code	NACE description
Motor vehicles and motorcycles	4511	Sale of cars and light motor vehicles
	4519	Sale of other motor vehicles
	4520	Maintenance and repair of motor vehicles
	4531	Wholesale trade of motor vehicle parts and accessories
	4532	Retail trade of motor vehicle parts and accessories
	4540	Sale, maintenance and repair of motorcycles and related parts and accessories
Household cultural and recreation goods	4649	Wholesale of other household goods
	4761	Retail sale of books in specialised stores
	4762	Retail sale of newspapers and stationery in specialised stores
	4763	Retail sale of music and video recordings in specialised stores
	4764	Retail sale of sporting equipment in specialised stores
	4765	Retail sale of games and toys in specialised stores
Furniture, lighting equipment and other manufacturing n.e.c	4690	Non-specialised wholesale trade
	4615	Agents involved in the sale of furniture, household goods, hardware and ironmongery
	4647	Wholesale of furniture, carpets and lighting equipment
	4665	Wholesale of office furniture
	4719	Other retail sale in non-specialised stores
	4753	Retail sale of carpets, rugs, wall and floor coverings in specialised stores
	4759	Retail sale of furniture, lighting equipment and other household articles in specialised stores
	4778	Other retail sale of new goods in specialised stores

ORGANISATION FOR ECONOMIC CO-OPERATION AND DEVELOPMENT

The OECD is a unique forum where governments work together to address the economic, social and environmental challenges of globalisation. The OECD is also at the forefront of efforts to understand and to help governments respond to new developments and concerns, such as corporate governance, the information economy and the challenges of an ageing population. The Organisation provides a setting where governments can compare policy experiences, seek answers to common problems, identify good practice and work to co-ordinate domestic and international policies.

The OECD member countries are: Australia, Austria, Belgium, Canada, Chile, the Czech Republic, Denmark, Estonia, Finland, France, Germany, Greece, Hungary, Iceland, Ireland, Israel, Italy, Japan, Korea, Latvia, Luxembourg, Mexico, the Netherlands, New Zealand, Norway, Poland, Portugal, the Slovak Republic, Slovenia, Spain, Sweden, Switzerland, Turkey, the United Kingdom and the United States. The European Union takes part in the work of the OECD.

OECD Publishing disseminates widely the results of the Organisation's statistics gathering and research on economic, social and environmental issues, as well as the conventions, guidelines and standards agreed by its members.

OECD PUBLISHING, 2, rue André-Pascal, 75775 PARIS CEDEX 16
(42 2017 32 1 P) ISBN 978-92-64-27905-6 – 2017

www.ingramcontent.com/pod-product-compliance
Lightning Source LLC
Chambersburg PA
CBHW041324210926
51847CB00003B/40
9789264279056